EssexWorks

D0541994

is **NOT**
MAD
at **YOU**

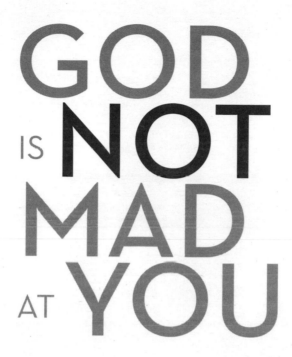

GOD IS NOT MAD AT YOU

You Can Experience Real Love,
Acceptance & Guilt-free Living

JOYCE MEYER

HODDER &
STOUGHTON

First published in Great Britain in 2013 by Hodder & Stoughton
An Hachette UK company

Published in association with FaithWords
Hachette Book Group
237 Park Avenue
New York, NY 10017

1

A CIP catalogue record for this title is available from the British Library

ISBN 978 1 444 74996 0
eBook ISBN 978 1 444 74997 7

Printed and bound in the UK by Clays Ltd, St Ives plc

Hodder & Stoughton policy is to use papers that are natural, renewable and recyclable
products and made from wood grown in sustainable forests. The logging and
manufacturing processes are expected to conform to the environmental
regulations of the country of origin.

Hodder & Stoughton Ltd
338 Euston Road
London NW1 3BH

www.hodderfaith.com

CONTENTS

Introduction	vii
Chapter 1: Is God Angry?	1
Chapter 2: Performance Mentality	14
Chapter 3: Perfectionism and Approval	22
Chapter 4: The Anxiety and Anger of the Perfectionist	35
Chapter 5: Father Issues	49
Chapter 6: The Pain of Rejection	63
Chapter 7: Learning to See Clearly	76
Chapter 8: Guilt and Shame	87
Chapter 9: Religion	102
Chapter 10: Sad, Mad, or Glad?	114
Chapter 11: Be the Person God Meant You to Be	127
Chapter 12: Developing Your Potential	139
Chapter 13: Mercy Is Greater Than Anger	149
Chapter 14: Mercy Can Never Be Earned	160
Chapter 15: Amazing Grace	172
Chapter 16: Greater Grace	184
Chapter 17: Run to God, Not from Him!	194
Chapter 18: What Shall We Do About Sin?	203
Chapter 19: Getting Comfortable with God	213
Chapter 20: Spiritual Growth	223

One day I put a post on Facebook that simply said, "God's not mad at you," and the response we received at the ministry was overwhelming. In just a few hours, thousands of people responded favorably. Many of them said, "That is exactly what I needed to hear today." They obviously were people who were afraid that God was mad at them and desperately needed to be assured that He wasn't.

Through my own experience in my relationship with God, and through ministering to other people, I have come to believe that a large percentage of people, either vaguely or perhaps even clearly, believe that God is mad at them. This belief prevents us from receiving His love, mercy, grace and forgiveness. It leaves us fearful, lacking confidence and feeling guilty. Even though we may ask for God's forgiveness for our sins and failures, we often still feel that God is disappointed and angry because we are less than He wants and expects us to be.

Where does this concept of God come from? Perhaps from an angry parent who was difficult to please. Or the pain of rejection from parents or friends who did not know how to give unconditional love. Perhaps it came from church! From religious teaching that offered us rules and regulations to follow, and implied that we would be unacceptable to God if we did not follow them. We wanted to be good, we tried to be good, but when we discovered—as everyone does—that we constantly fail, we silently accepted the message that we were a major disappointment to God, deserving of His anger. We did however, continue to try to change and behave better because we love God, and we definitely don't want Him to be angry with us.

In this condition we are faced with a lifetime of disappointment because anyone who attempts to serve God under the law (rules and regulations) is doomed to disappointment according to the apostle Paul:

> *And all who depend on the Law [who are seeking to be justified by obedience to the Law of rituals] are under a curse and doomed to disappointment.*
>
> Galatians 3:10

In our relationships with our parents or other people, we may have had to perform in a certain way in order to earn their love, but God's love is unconditional, and is freely offered to all who will receive it by faith.

You will learn in this book that although God does get angry at sin, wickedness and evil, He is not an angry God. God hates sin, but He loves sinners! He is "good, and ready to forgive [our trespasses, sending them away, letting them go completely and forever]." He is abundant in mercy and filled with loving-kindness (Psalm 86:5). Let me be clear: God does not and never will approve of sin, but He does love sinners and will continue to work with us toward positive change in our lives. God never stops loving us for even one second of our lives, and it is because of His great love that He refuses to leave us alone, lost and abandoned in sin. He meets us where we are and helps us get to where we need to be.

The Bible is a record of sin, deceit, immorality of every kind, disobedience, hypocrisy and God's amazing grace and love. The heroes we admire were people just like us. They failed miserably at times, they sinned regularly, and yet they found love, acceptance, forgiveness and mercy to be the free gifts of God. His love drew them into intimate relationship with Him, empowered them to do great things, and taught them to enjoy the life that He has provided.

Since they experienced that acceptance, I believe we can experience it, too, if we will make a decision to believe what God's Word says to us instead of what we think, feel or hear from others. We should make sure that our beliefs are in agreement with God's Word, and not merely a fabrication of misled thinking. One might believe that God does not love him and is angry with him, but that is not what God's Word says; therefore, the wrong thinking should be rejected as a counterfeit, and what God says should be accepted by faith without question. God has given us His Word that we might always have the truth available to us. It is impossible for us to live a life of deception if we make God's Word our source of all truth and believe it above all else.

You may think, "There is absolutely no reason for God to love me," and you are absolutely right. But God does love you. He chooses to do so, and because He is God, He has every right to do so. The Bible says that He planned to love us and to adopt us as His own children because it was His will, it pleased Him, and was His kind intent (Ephesians 1:5). God loves us because He wants to, not because we deserve it. I would like to suggest that you stop reading for a few minutes and repeat out loud several times, "God loves me because He wants to, not because I deserve it." Each time you say it, take a moment and let it sink into your consciousness. Being conscious and aware of God's love is the beginning of all healing and restoration. It is the source of all righteousness, peace and joy. We should learn to be God-conscious instead of sin-conscious. Focus on God's goodness instead of our failures. Focusing on our weaknesses only gives them more strength and power over us.

To live in the reality that God is not mad at us is the most free-ing truth that we will ever find. Knowing that we will sin, prob-ably every day, and that God knows that and has already decided to forgive us eliminates the fear of failure. The beautiful truth is that when we no longer focus on our sin, we find that we do it less and less. As we focus on God's goodness instead of being afraid of our weaknesses, we become more and more like Jesus. God, in Christ, has totally taken care of the problem of sin. To be sure, God commands us not to sin, but He knew that we would due to the weakness of our flesh, so He took care of the problem by sending us His Son Jesus as the sacrifice and payment for our sins. Jesus paid for everything that we have done or ever will do wrong, and He opened up a new way for us to live and serve God. Not in fear or guilt, but in freedom, love and intimacy.

God is determined to have intimate relationship with each of us, and the only way He can do that is if He extends grace, mercy and forgiveness to us continually. The only way we can have that relationship with Him is if we learn to continually receive His grace, forgiveness and mercy.

In case you are wondering, you have not already received too much mercy in your life. There is still an abundant amount avail-able to you, and there will be as long as you live. God's mercy is new every day! It is a gift and can only be enjoyed if it is received freely.

As you read this book, I pray that you will receive God's grace, favor, love, mercy, forgiveness and the glorious truth that God's not mad at you! May you live boldly and be all God intends you to be, and live in the fullness of the joy and beauty that you were created for. Form the habit of meditating on and confessing this truth: "God is not mad at me."

GOD
IS **NOT**
MAD
AT YOU

CHAPTER 1

Is God Angry?

The Lord is merciful and gracious, slow to anger and plen-
teous in mercy and loving-kindness.
    He will not always chide or be contending, neither will
He keep His anger forever or hold a grudge.

Psalm 103:8–9

A woman I know tells a story about the time she burnt out the
engine of her father's car, which he had loaned her when she was
in college. It was the end of semester break, and she was going
to head back to school on the bus, a seven-hour ride with a lot
of stops on the way. Ellen had been given a lot of Christmas
gifts that were bulky, including a down-filled comforter and a
new desktop computer. Her dad told her that rather than deal
with so many big items on the bus, she could drive his car back
to school and return it the next time she came home for a visit.
What a gift!

The trip back to college was a breeze. Ellen parked the car in
a safe spot and planned to drive home and return it within a few
weeks. In the meantime, every now and then she'd drive to the
grocery store or the mall. Pretty soon, she was taking her friends
on short trips here and there just for fun.

On one of those trips, Ellen noticed a red light blinking on the
dashboard. She didn't think it was anything serious; after all, her

father took great care of the car and it was in good condition. She just kept driving.

Soon she noticed some smoke coming out of the hood and decided she'd better get the car back to campus. Next came a few loud sputters, and then the engine died. When the tow-truck driver arrived, it didn't take him long to figure out the problem: That red light on the dash was an oil indicator. Ellen had neglected to check out the light, and now the engine was beyond repair.

A few days later, when her father arrived (in his remaining car) and she met him at the gas station where the car had been towed, Ellen was terrified. She had abused a privilege and ignored a simple warning. There was no excuse for her neglect, and now she'd destroyed her father's car. She knew he was furious, and there was no defense for her behavior. Ellen told her father how sorry she was for her carelessness, but he just told her to sit in the car while he assessed the damage.

After learning that the car was now worthless, Ellen's father arranged for the gas station to dispose of it. He actually had to pay them to take it off his hands! Now it was time for Ellen to face his wrath.

As they drove away from the trashed car, her father asked Ellen, "Where's the best restaurant in town?" That was the last thing she'd expected to hear, but she directed him to it. As they sat at the table and looked at the menu, Ellen couldn't think about food. Fortunately, her father ordered for both of them: broiled trout almondine. They sat in silence while they waited for their food, every minute feeling like an hour.

When the trout arrived, Ellen's father said to her, "Tonight I want to teach you a lesson that you'll never forget." She knew she deserved whatever she got. Would he make her pay him for the car? That would take forever. Would he yell at her? Maybe he would just tell her how disappointed he was in her. In some ways, that would be the worst punishment.

Then he took his knife and fork in hand and said, "I'm going to teach you how to remove the skeleton from cooked trout." Not a word was said about the car that night—or ever again.

Ellen's father had been angry about her behavior—who wouldn't be? But he also knew that Ellen had learned her lesson without retribution from him. Ellen is nearly sixty now, and her father died many years ago. But she tells this story as if it happened last week, and she is still in awe of her father's forgiveness. His grace made a greater impact on her than his punishment ever would have.

God's Word says that He behaves the same way toward us that Ellen's father did toward her.

> The Lord your God is in the midst of you, a Mighty One, a Savior [Who saves]! He will rejoice over you with joy; He will rest [in silent satisfaction] and in His love He will be silent and make no mention [of past sins, or even recall them]; He will exult over you with singing.
>
> Zephaniah 3:17

To be sure, there are many examples in the Bible of our heavenly Father getting angry, but that does not mean that He is an angry God. He does at times get angry at sin, disobedience and rebellion. But He is slow to anger, abundant in mercy and always ready to forgive. All of our sins—past, present and future—have already been forgiven. This took place when Jesus died on the cross. All we need to do is believe it and receive it any time we fail. Ask and receive that your joy may be full (John 16:24).

Don't make the mistake of spending your life believing that God is mad at you, when the forgiveness you need is available at all times. Speak freely with God about your sins. He already knows all about them, but bringing them out into the open and letting nothing remain hidden between you and God is very liberating. It is awesome to realize that we can talk freely to God about absolutely anything and that He understands and does not judge us. That doesn't mean that He approves of sinful behavior, but He does understand the weakness in our flesh (Hebrews 4:15–16), and His power enables us to overcome it.

There are many instances recorded in the Bible of God's anger blazing against the Israelites because of their complaining, disobedience, and worship of idols and false gods. But the amazing thing to me is how quick God was to completely forgive them and restore all of His benefits to them as soon as they turned away from their wickedness and back to Him.

This happened over and over again throughout the Old Testament. It is truly astonishing how often Israel served God and enjoyed His abundant blessings and then turned away in rebellion and disobedience to worship idols and to please their own selves. It is even more astonishing how quickly and freely God took them back, forgave them and restored them to their former prosperity when they turned back to Him with sincere and repentant hearts. It is very evident from the history of these people, who were God's chosen ones, that He is faithful and always ready to forgive and restore.

Perhaps you think that God is angry with you. Surely, if God was quick to forgive people who turned entirely away from Him and worshipped idols, He is more than ready to forgive you and me for our sins.

As far as the east is from the west, so far has He removed our transgressions from us.

As a father loves and pities his children, so the Lord loves and pities those who fear Him [with reverence, worship, and awe].

For He knows our frame, He [earnestly] remembers and imprints [on His heart] that we are dust.

Psalm 103:12–14

We are reminded in these Scripture verses that God understands our weaknesses. He knows that we will at times succumb to temptations and wrong behavior, but He is also a compassionate, loving Father who stands ready to forgive everything. The very fact that we cannot do everything right is why God sent Jesus to pay the price for our redemption.

Hosea Marries a Harlot

The story of the prophet Hosea is an extraordinary picture of God's amazing love and deep commitment to the children of Israel. God commanded Hosea to marry a harlot named Gomer and to have children with her. This was intended to be a living example to the Israelites of God's faithfulness in the face of their unfaithfulness.

Hosea and Gomer had three children who were named by God. Their names were prophetic. In other words, they were intended to be a message for the children of Israel. The first was named Jezreel, which signified God's judgment on the ruling king Jeroboam. The second was named Lo-Ruhamah, meaning "not pitied," which conveyed the message that God was about to withdraw His mercy from Israel. The third child was named Lo-Ammi and it meant "Not-my-people." The names of these children were a prophetic reminder to Israel that God was displeased with their unfaithfulness.

Gomer was unfaithful to Hosea, and her infidelity was a symbol of Israel's unfaithfulness to her covenant relationship with God. Instead of responding to God's goodness with love and gratitude, the Israelites used the crops God had blessed them with as offerings to idols. They were unfaithful to God just as Gomer was unfaithful to Hosea.

Even though Gomer was unfaithful to Hosea, God commanded him to take her back again and love her.

> Then said the Lord to me, Go again, love [the same] woman [Gomer] who is beloved of a paramour and is an adulteress, even as the Lord loves the children of Israel, though they turn to other gods and love cakes of raisins [used in the sacrificial feasts in idol worship].
>
> Hosea 3:1

This was intended to show God's commitment and everlasting love for His people. Although God was angry at the Israelites for their amazingly stupid behavior, He never stopped loving them. He intended to deal with them in a way that would eventually draw them back to Him. So we see that even in our sin, God devises ways to draw us back into a loving relationship with Him. God is not ever going to give up on us!

> Therefore return to your God! Hold fast to love and mercy, to righteousness and justice, and wait [expectantly] for your God continually!
>
> Hosea 12:6

All God required in order to restore the Israelites' relationship with Him was for them to return to Him and repent of their iniquity. He wanted them to be sorry for what they had done, turn away from their sin and turn back to Him.

If you have served God at some time and walked away from Him to have an affair with the world, surely this story gives you hope that God is waiting with open arms to receive you back. Yes, God does get angry, but His nature is to forgive and restore.

God's Anger Is Different from Ours

When we get angry with people, it is usually because they did something to us that we don't like, or they didn't do something we believe they should have. Our anger is always due to someone hurting us. When God gets angry, it is not because of what we are doing to Him. It is because of what we are doing to ourselves by not following His ways. You might even say that His anger is for us, not against us. God's love is everlasting, and even His anger and displeasure are intended to drive us away from sin and back to Him.

Although we often resist God's commandments because we think they are hard to follow or will prevent us from doing what we want to do, we are wrong. Everything that God commands us to do—or not to do—is for our good. Our obedience to Him will give us the life we truly desire. The Bible is a record of how blessed people are when they follow God, and how miserable and wretched they are when they don't. God said it very simply in His Word:

> *If you will listen diligently to the voice of the Lord your God,*
> *being watchful to do all His commandments which I command*

*you this day, the Lord your God will set you high above all
the nations of the earth.*

*And all these blessings shall come upon you and over-
take you.*

Deuteronomy 28:1–2

We don't need to chase blessings, because they will chase us
if we will simply do what God asks us to do. Most people are so
busy chasing blessings and trying to obtain what they think they
want out of life that they fail to obey God. Their actions are coun-
terproductive and will never produce the result they desire. If we
will put God first in our lives, He will add all the things we need
and desire (Matthew 6:33).

*But if you will not obey the voice of the Lord your God, being
watchful to do all His commandments and His statutes which
I command you this day, then all these curses shall come
upon you and overtake you.*

Deuteronomy 28:15

In the Scriptures above we see the law of sowing and reaping
in operation. Follow God and reap good things; rebel against God
and reap a harvest of bad things. The extraordinary, good news,
though, is that if you have sown bad seed (disobedience), you
need not be afraid, because all you need to do is begin sowing
good seed (obedience) and you will see God's goodness in your
life.

I know a young man who is eighteen years old, who was raised
in a good Christian home, but has chosen to go his own way and
do every wrong thing that he can possibly do. It almost seems that
he is bent on self-destruction but is oblivious to what he is doing.

His parents are not angry with him; they are sad for him. They are angry at the evil that has persuaded him to go in the wrong direction, but they are praying and waiting for his return to God and to them. With a few sincere words of repentance from him, they will receive him back without reproach or condemnation. If a parent can do that, how much more can our perfect God do it!

You don't have to live in fear that God is mad at you! Look away from your sinful behavior and look to God instead.

A Bigger Problem Than Sin?

I think Scripture proves that our unbelief is a much larger problem than our sins. Sin can always be forgiven for those who will repent and believe, but when unbelief exists, God's hands are tied when it comes to helping us.

The Word of God teaches that it will be done to us according to how we believe. In other words, when I believe that God is angry with me because of my imperfections, no matter how much He loves me and wants to forgive and restore me, I will not receive it because I don't believe it.

Our unbelief is a tragedy when it comes to God's good plan for our lives. He longs for us to believe Him, to come to Him with simple childlike faith and trust what He says to us in His Word.

God called Moses to bring deliverance to His people. It was actually something that Moses had longed for, yet when God finally said the time had come for Moses to act, he refused to believe that he could do what God was asking him to do. Moses made one excuse after another until finally the Bible records that God's anger "blazed against Moses" (Exodus 4:14).

Simply put, God got angry because Moses would not believe! He eventually did obey God, and of course God was faithful.

We learn from the apostle Paul in the book of Hebrews that the Israelites were never allowed to enter God's rest as they traveled through the wilderness due to their hardness of heart and refusal to believe His promises. Unbelief makes us miserable and steals every blessing that God desires for us. It also makes God angry. He so much wants us to be blessed in every way that when we do things that prevent His blessings, it makes Him angry. It is a holy anger, not a selfish anger as we experience in our humanity. It is important for us to remember that God's anger is directed toward our sinful behavior rather than toward us. I may hate something one of my children does, but I always love my child.

If you feel guilty right now and are afraid that God is mad at you, then you are miserable. But your misery can be immediately changed to peace and joy by simply believing God's Word. Believe that God loves you and that He is ready to show you mercy and forgive you completely. Believe that God has a good plan for your life. Believe that God is not mad at you!

Sinners in the Hands of an Angry God

Jonathan Edwards, one of the greatest preachers the world has ever known, delivered a sermon entitled *Sinners in the Hands of an Angry God*. It is considered by many to be the most famous sermon ever preached. The response from those who heard the message was nothing short of amazing. They often cried out during Edwards's preaching, asking how they might be spared, and flocked to the altar for salvation. It was a frightening message about God's anger at sin and the dangers of being sent to Hell.

I don't mean what I am about to say as a criticism of Edwards' message, because it is evident that God used it in a mighty way. But I do wonder why people respond to God's anger more quickly than they do to His love and mercy. To be honest, it makes me sad. I would much rather my children respond to my love than to a threat of punishment if they don't obey me, and I am sure you are the same way with your children. I can't help but believe that God is the same way with His children. Surely, He doesn't want to have to frighten us into obedience through threats of our ending up in Hell. It may work in the lives of some people, and I suppose it is better than nothing, but I cannot believe it is God's preferred method of dealing with us.

I also wonder if people who are frightened into repentance by the thought of eternal punishment continue with God, or if some perhaps go back to their old ways. I doubt that a good relationship can be built on fear.

Love is stronger than fear, and if we respond to God's love, it will cast out all of our fears. We can respond obediently to God because we know He loves us rather than because we are afraid of punishment.

> There is no fear in love [dread does not exist], but full-grown (complete, perfect) love turns fear out of doors and expels every trace of terror! For fear brings with it the thought of punishment, and [so] he who is afraid has not reached the full maturity of love [is not yet grown into love's complete perfection].
>
> 1 John 4:18

I wasted many years living with a vague fear that God was angry with me, and it wasn't until I received His love by faith that I was released from that burden. I believed that God loved me in some sort of general, impersonal way, but I did not know the fierce, fiery, all-consuming love that God has for His children.

Fortunately, over the years I have come to know that amazing, passionate love, and it has truly delivered me. I now know that God is not angry with me; He isn't even annoyed with me! And it isn't because of my wonderful self; it is simply because He's in love with me. I'm no longer afraid to face Him just as I am.

God wants to do the same thing for you, and you need not fear His anger even another moment. God loves you perfectly and unconditionally *right now*! Believe it, receive it and let it deliver you from all fear.

I think it is insulting to God when we believe He is angry and wrathful, just waiting to punish each of our misdeeds. If we spend our time believing that God is angry with us, we are focusing on what we have done wrong, instead of what God has done right in sending His Son to pay for our sins. For sure, we all sin, and God doesn't like it, but I believe that He is easier to get along with than we might think He is. He is good, kind, merciful and slow to anger, forgiving, faithful and just. He is to be loved, worshipped, praised, thanked, and adored. And yes, God is to be feared, but it is a reverential awe and respect that He wants us to have for Him, not a sick, debilitating, tormenting fear that destroys intimacy and relationship with Him. He wants us to fear Him, but not to be afraid of Him; there is a huge difference between the two.

Perhaps you need an entirely new view of God. A biblical view, not a worldview as many have today. I can assure you that no matter what you have done or what you may be doing right now that is wrong and sinful, God does love you, and although He may be angry at your ways, He has never stopped and never will stop loving you!

If you receive His love right in the midst of your imperfection, it will empower you to change your ways with His help. Fear does not help us truly change. It may provoke us to control our behavior for a time, but unless we are changed inwardly, we will never change permanently. We will always revert to our sin in times of stress and weakness. But if we receive God's love even while we are still sinners, our gratitude for His great mercy will make us want to please Him rather than be afraid of Him.

CHAPTER 2

Performance Mentality

Our best performances are so stained with sin that it's hard to know whether they are good works or bad works.

Charles Spurgeon

Our fear that God is angry with us is rooted in the fear that we have not performed as expected. We did not get an A on our spiritual test, we fell short of our goal, we lost our temper, and now we are disappointed with ourselves, and we are sure that God is disappointed, too.

The truth is that God already knew that we wouldn't perform as expected when He chose to love us. God is never surprised by our failures! As long as we are on what I call the "performance/acceptance" treadmill, we will inevitably suffer with disappointment in ourselves and an unhealthy fear that God is more than likely angry. But God has not asked us to perform; He asks us to believe.

Our first goal is to develop a relationship with God based on His love for us and ours for Him. When our relationship with God is a solid foundation in our lives, we can go on attempting good works that are spirit led, but they will be done out of desire, not fear. We will be free to do the best we can, and not get stressed-out about our imperfections. We are not to get out of bed each day and try to perform for God and people in order to get their approval, applause and acceptance. We should have the goal of loving God and people, and of doing the best we can for no reason except that we love God and sincerely want to do the right things.

It is time to break free from the trap of doing right to be rewarded and learn to do right because it is right. God does reward us, but our motive for serving Him must be love and love alone. And we cannot respond to God in love until we are fully convinced that He loves us unconditionally.

> *We love Him, because He first loved us*
>
> 1 John 4:19

God is not like the baseball coach who is disappointed in us when we strike out in the last inning and cause the team to lose the game. God knew that we would strike out before He let us play the game. The Bible shows us that God knows our faults and loves us anyway. The beauty of grace is that *"while we were still sinners, Christ died for us"* (Romans 5:8).

God has already accepted us; therefore, we don't have to try to perform in order to earn His acceptance. We are made acceptable in the Beloved (Jesus) (Ephesians 2:4–6; Romans 5:19). God views us as acceptable through Jesus Christ. When God looks at anyone who has accepted Jesus as Savior and Lord, He sees the perfection of Jesus, not the imperfection of the individual. Once we have received Jesus as our Savior, the only thing that matters is who we are in Christ—not our performance record. In and of ourselves, we are nothing and can do nothing perfectly right. But by virtue of being in Christ, by faith we can do anything God wants us to do, and do it to His satisfaction. God doesn't require our perfection... He requires our faith.

Get Off the Treadmill

Is your mentality, "I owe, I owe, so off to work I go"? It was mine for many long years. Each day when I woke up, I felt I had to pay for all my sins and mistakes of the day before, so I formulated a plan for how good I would be, hoping to work my way back into God's pleasure and favor. During that time, I regularly attended a church that clearly taught that salvation is by grace and not by works. I said I believed it, but I didn't apply it to my life.

Even though I did some things right each day, I also did many things wrong that overshadowed the little bit I did that was right, so I never got ahead. The next day I still owed for the day before and had to get back on the treadmill once again. By the end of each day, I was spiritually, mentally, physically and emotionally worn-out from trying to please God. And it made me grouchy and not very enjoyable to be around.

I did not yet have revelation of what Jesus said in the book of Matthew:

> Come to Me, all you who labor and are heavy-laden and overburdened, and I will cause you to rest. [I will ease and relieve and refresh your souls.]
>
> Matthew 11:28

My translation of this verse of Scripture would go something like this: "Get off the treadmill of performance/acceptance and just come to Me. Trust My love for you and be assured that you are not accepted because of what you can do, but because of what I have done for you. Breathe a sigh of relief and don't be stressed-out by your faults."

How Much Is Wrong with You?

If you made a list of everything that is wrong with you, how long would it be? I can assure you that even if you wrote down everything you could think of, and even if you asked family and friends for their additions, you would still miss a lot of things. God knows them all, and His desire is that we stop counting. If we reached up with a cutting tool and cut the power line coming into our house one time, we would be without power. If we cut it ten times, we would be without power. Whether we sin often or rarely, we have still cut the power line from us to God, and we all need Jesus to restore it. Even if you think you are better than someone else you know, it doesn't matter because God is not counting. According to God's Word, if we are depending on the law to justify us and we are guilty of one thing, then we are guilty of all. Fortunately, He offers us an opportunity to live under grace and not the law.

> *For whosoever keeps the Law [as a] whole but stumbles and offends in one [single instance] has become guilty of [breaking] all of it.*
>
> James 2:10

I knew a woman who made a list of everything she wanted to accomplish each day. She delighted in checking things off her list because it gave her a feeling of succeeding. However, when she had things left on her list, it made her feel like a failure and she usually became angry with herself. She was always counting things. Pieces of clothing to be ironed, chores left to be done, length of time it took her to do things, et cetera. I remember counting how long I prayed and keeping precise records of how much of the Bible I read each day as if my right standing with God increased or decreased because of it. I have been delivered from counting, the woman I am speaking of has been delivered from counting, and I pray that you, too, will be delivered from counting what you have done right or wrong. God's grace sets us free from counting! Love takes no account of the evil done to it, and it keeps no records of wrong (1 Corinthians 13:5). God keeps short accounts! When we post a debit (a sin) to our account, He posts a credit (forgiveness and mercy). In Christ our account balance that we owe God is always zero! It always says, "Paid in full."

The law requires us to count and keep precise records of our sins, and to pay for them with sacrifices. Those who live under the law never stop feeling guilty. Their sin may be covered by their sacrifice of good works, loss of joy, or guilt, but it is never completely removed. It is always lurking in the shadows accusing them. If, however, we live under grace (God's undeserved favor), we have the assurance that even though we are guilty of many things, we are freely and completely forgiven, and we are in right standing with God. God is not angry with us!

Peter said that Jesus died—the innocent for the guilty—that He might bring us to God (1 Peter 3:18). Are you ready to stop counting and just go to God? When you make mistakes don't run from God and hide in fear thinking He is mad, but instead run *to* Him to fix what is wrong. When a baby is learning to walk and falls down, he runs to Mom and Dad for comfort and is comforted and encouraged to try again. I have recently spent a lot of time with my two youngest grandsons. As I watch them throughout the day, when they get into trouble or get hurt, they immediately run to Mom and Dad. I've noticed that they don't ever run away from their parents; they run to them, or they sit on the floor with uplifted arms, asking to be picked up. Jesus died so that you and I could run to God every single time we fall. Surely such a costly gift should not go to waste.

On rare occasions when my dog has an accident and poos on the floor (which is usually during a storm), she hangs her head and cowers until she hears me say in a loving voice, "Come here." I can assure you that once she hears those words, she has not one ounce of guilt left. She returns to her play just as if she had done nothing wrong. She plays and I clean up the mess! Is it possible that God is offering us the same grace? Yes it is! To keep her from going back and doing it again, I spray PetZyme™ on it. We have something much more powerful than PetZyme™ to remove our poo stains—we have the blood of Jesus Christ in which we are washed and made completely clean (Hebrews 10:14,17–19).

Jesus has completely cleansed us. He has forgiven and canceled our sins and there is no longer any offering that can be made. We don't have to work to pay because we don't owe. Our debt has been paid in full by the blood, suffering and sacrifice of Jesus!

What Are You Offering God as Payback?

If you have been on the performance/acceptance treadmill, what are you offering God as payback for your sins? Are you sacrificing your enjoyment of life? Do you feel undeserving and guilty when you relax and try to have fun? Do you carry a burden of guilt, condemnation and shame with you everywhere that you go? Do you work excessively, feeling you are more acceptable when you do? These were my preferred methods of self-punishment and I thought you might recognize some of them. Large percentages of the crowds that I minister to, when asked, admit that they feel guilty when they try to relax. If you feel that, too, it is *not God* making you feel that way! He has commanded us to rest as part of His divine rhythm of life. Work, rest, worship and play are all vital for wholeness. If we leave any facet out, we will not be whole individuals, and we will always feel that we are deprived and missing something.

We cannot do enough right to make up for our wrong. We cannot pay God back; He doesn't want us to try to.

> *None of them can by any means redeem [either himself or] his brother, nor give to God a ransom for him:*
> *For the ransom of a life is too costly, and [the price one can pay] can never suffice.*
>
> Psalm 49:7–8

In some places, the Grand Canyon is nine miles wide. I could jump maybe three feet, Dave could jump eight to twelve feet and a broad jumper could jump twenty-four to twenty-six feet—but we are all very short of nine miles, and very dead without someone to save us.

Thank God we have been saved and no longer have to struggle to make a jump that is impossible to make.

Judah Smith tells a wonderful story about his young son that makes a crucial point.

> *My four-year-old son, Zion, plays soccer. Actually, that's overstating it. He runs around a field with a bunch of other four-year-olds, and once in a while someone accidentally bumps into the ball.*
> *The other day I was at practice—not a game, just practice—and the ball squirted out of the pack and toward*

the opposing goal. Then I saw Zion break out of the herd, chasing the ball, and something came over me.

Now, soccer practice for four-year-olds is essentially a cheap substitute for daycare, so I was the only parent on the sidelines. But when Zion had a chance to score a goal, you would have thought it was the World Cup of preschoolers.

I ran down the sidelines, screaming, "Kick the ball, Zion, kick the ball!" The coach probably thought I needed therapy, but I didn't care. This was my son, and he was awesome.

Then, a miracle; he kicked the ball, and it bounced off his ankle and into the goal. Next thing he knew, I was swooping him up onto my shoulders, parading him around the field and proclaiming how great he was.

And I was sincere.

In this instance, Zion performed well, and his dad was immensely proud. But I know Judah Smith's character, and I know that he will love and accept his son equally if he totally fails at the next practice or game. As good parents, we are not up and down in our commitment to love our children.

Some of us are way too emotional—too up and down. I did something good today and God is pleased. I sinned, and God's mad at me. Have you ever heard of the foreknowledge of God? He knows—and has always known—about our future failures. If He loves us now, knowing what we'll do wrong tomorrow, why are we doubting? Embrace grace and move on!

It is very good news that we don't have to wear ourselves out daily trying to manifest a perfect performance so God can love us. He is going to love us either way, so let's just do the best we can out of a heart of love for God, and trust His mercy for our failures.

CHAPTER 3

Perfectionism and Approval

No one is perfect…that's why pencils have erasers.

Author Unknown

When Charlie was a child, each autumn, his dad gave him the chore of raking up the leaves. It was a difficult job for a young boy, taking hours to complete, but one he did without argument. At the completion of his task, he would say, "Daddy, you're going to love it; the yard looks amazing!"

Every fall, his dad had the same response at the conclusion of his yard inspection. "It looks good, son, but you missed some leaves over there…and a few over there…and there are a few more by the gate." Charlie's dad was a perfectionist and Charlie never felt that he measured up to his dad's expectations.

Perfectionism is a cold and sterile symptom of a legalistic mind-set. Jesus scolded the Pharisees when He said, "They tie up heavy loads, hard to bear, and place them on men's shoulders, but they themselves will not lift a finger to help bear them" (Matthew 23:4).

The Pharisees were great at making others feel as if they didn't measure up. This is the opposite of grace, and perhaps that is why Jesus so vehemently opposed the Pharisees' behavior. Satan is The Accuser of the brethren, and he delights in trying to make us feel that we don't measure up to God's expectations.

God not only does not expect us to be perfect, but it is precisely *because* we are not and never will be perfect that He sent Jesus to save us and the Holy Spirit to help us in our daily life. If we could do it by ourselves, we would not need help. Jesus didn't come to make us perfect people with no flaws, but He came to forgive our imperfections and to wipe them away in God's sight. We actually are perfect through Jesus, but we can never be perfect in our own performance.

Jesus did say, "Be perfect even as your Father in heaven is perfect," (Matthew 5:48) but a study of the original language reveals that He meant that we should grow into complete maturity of godliness in mind and character. The thought of growing doesn't frighten or overwhelm me because it is a process that goes on all throughout our lives. I love to learn, to change and to grow. However, when I thought I was being commanded to "be perfect right now," I did feel frightened and it overwhelmed me because I knew that I wasn't perfect and didn't know how I ever could be. Now I know that I will still be growing even when Jesus returns to take me to heaven. God is not disappointed that we have not arrived at manifesting perfect behavior, but He does delight in finding us growing into maturity.

> *Striving for excellence motivates you; striving for perfection is demoralizing.*
>
> Harriet Braiker

We are called to be excellent, but God leaves flaws in even His choicest saints so that they will always need Him. I like to say that excellence is not perfection, but it is taking what you have to work with and doing the best you can with it, all the while trusting Jesus to fill in the gaps.

A Perfect Heart

Although I don't believe that we can have a perfect performance, I do believe that we can have a perfect heart toward God. That means that we love Him wholeheartedly, and we want to please Him and do what is right. When we receive Jesus as the perfect sacrifice for our sins, He gives us a new heart and puts His Spirit in us. The heart He gives us is a perfect heart. I like to say that He gives us a new "want to." He gives us a desire to please Him.

> *And I will give them one heart [a new heart] and I will put a new spirit within them; and I will take the stony [unnaturally hardened] heart out of their flesh, and will give them a heart of flesh [sensitive and responsive to the touch of their God].*
>
> Ezekiel 11:19

Do you love God? I believe you do, or you wouldn't be reading this book. If you don't have an intimate relationship of love with God, you are probably searching for one, and God is also pleased with your desire to know Him. There is a lot in life that I don't know, and a lot about God that I still don't completely understand, but I do know that I love Him as much as I possibly can at this point in my spiritual journey with Him. I hope to love Him more as I grow in Him, but for now I trust that my love for Him is what He delights in. You probably have that same kind of love for God, but you may not have come to the conclusion that your love for God is the most important thing to Him. God wants us to love Him because of Who He is, not just for what He does for us.

You may still be thinking that you have to perform perfectly in order to have His acceptance. If you believe that, it is a lie! The devil has lied to you, people have misled you, you are confused and the truth is that God does not expect us to be perfect in our performance.

Think about your children or other intimate relationships that you have. Do you really think that anyone you are in relationship with is going to be perfect all of the time? Of course you don't! I already know that there will be times when Dave or my children will disappoint me or fail to treat me just right, but I am committed to them for life, so I have already decided to forgive them. I may have to go through the process of forgiveness each time they hurt me, but ultimately I will forgive and we will go on in our relationship.

God has this same kind of commitment to His children, only His is even more perfect than ours as parents could ever be. God already knows that you and I won't manifest perfection and He has already decided to forgive us. Wow! That takes the pressure off, doesn't it? When Jesus died for our sins, paying the ransom to redeem us, He died not only for the sins we have committed in the past, but for every wrong thing we would ever do as long as we live. All of our sins are already forgiven, past, present and future, and all we need to do is admit them and thankfully receive God's forgiveness. We are safe in His arms and completely covered by His grace. All He really wants is for us to love Him and out of that love do the best we can to serve and obey Him. I am convinced that if I do the best I can each day, even though my best is still imperfect, God sees my heart and views me as perfect anyway because of His grace (undeserved favor and blessing).

In I Kings 11:4, we read that David had a perfect heart. Now if you know anything about David, you know that he was not perfect in his behavior. He committed murder and adultery, but God says that he had a perfect heart. Just try to wrap your religious brain around that! How could God say that David's heart was perfect? He could say it because David thoroughly repented of his sin, and although he sinned greatly, he never stopped loving God. He manifested weakness due to the temptations of the flesh, and yes, he was guilty and very wrong in his behavior. What he did not only hurt God, but hurt a lot of other people, too. David was an imperfect man with a perfect heart.

It is said of Amaziah, king of Judah, "He did right in the Lord's sight, but not with a perfect or blameless heart" (2 Chronicles 25:2). There are people who do right, but their heart is far from God. The Pharisees had a polished performance, but because of their pride, their hearts were filled with criticism and judgment. I believe that God is more delighted with someone who has a perfect heart and makes mistakes than He is with someone who follows the law to the letter but whose heart is not right.

If you ever want to be delivered from the tyranny of perfectionism, you will have to understand the difference between a perfect heart and a perfect performance. The story below taken from the website of the Sicklerville United Methodist Church shows how a flawed gift can be utterly perfect in the eyes of a parent.

"Picture a sunny, humid and very hot August Saturday afternoon. You are mowing your lawn. You are about three-quarters finished and you are perspiring greatly. Your five-year-old has been playing in the sandbox. As you turn to make another pass with the lawnmower, you see him standing in front of you with a glass filled with ice and water. As your eyes meet, he lifts the glass toward you offering its cold refreshment. You turn off the lawnmower and reach for the glass. As you take it, you notice the sandbox sand is mixed in with the ice, clippings of grass are floating on top and dirty droplets of water are running down the sides of the glass. That is a picture of Christian perfection and of what Jesus meant when He said, 'Be perfect even as my Father is perfect.' Was that ice water absolutely perfect? Not at all; it had grass, sand and dirt floating in it. What made the glass of ice water perfect? It was a pure, genuine, sincere and loving heart of a little boy wanting to do something kind and loving for his father."

The Tyranny of the Oughts and Shoulds

We conducted a survey at our office, asking our employees what one of their greatest concerns was in their walk with God. The number one response was, "When can I know that I am doing enough?"

Perfectionism is fueled with the tyranny of the *shoulds* and *oughts*. It is the constant nagging feeling of never doing well enough or being good enough. We ought to be doing so-and-so, or at least more of it, and should be better than we are. We should pray better, read the Bible more and be kinder and more patient. We should be less selfish, more loving and on and on. We never run out of things on our list to make us dissatisfied with ourselves. This feeling haunts us in all areas of life, but more in our spiritual life than any other area. We instinctively want to be pleasing to God, and we are deeply afraid that we aren't. We believe that God is mad at us!

I grew up in a home with an angry father who was impossible to please. I spent every waking moment trying to please him, but no matter what I did, I lived with the gnawing feeling that he was probably still mad at me.

Perfectionists usually have low self-esteem, and they hope that more perfection in their performance will allow them to feel better about themselves. If we never feel quite good enough about ourselves, then it is easy to believe that God is not satisfied with us either. We should learn to love ourselves, and to not be against ourselves, rejecting ourselves, or even worse, hating ourselves. Learning to love yourself is the essence of receiving God's love. It is the ointment that brings healing to your wounded soul. Until we receive God's love and learn to love ourselves because of it, we will remain sick in our souls and live dysfunctional lives.

I well remember how I struggled to be strong and good at all times and continually felt that I did not measure up to God's expectations. I can truthfully say that I went through years of agony before I finally heard God whisper in my heart, "Joyce, it is okay for you to have weaknesses." I am sure that He had tried to teach me that previously but I was unable to hear it due to the wrong thinking I had. God wasn't telling me to try to be weak, but He was letting me know that He understood that I was, and that He wasn't angry with me because of it.

When God told me that it was okay for me to have some weaknesses it sounded too good to be true. I immediately began a Bible study of the word "weakness," and I discovered that Jesus actually understands our weaknesses (Hebrews 4:15). He understands them because He took on human flesh in order to identify with us, and He was tempted in every respect just as we are; while He never sinned, He is not shocked when we fail. I am certainly not saying that we should not work with the Holy Spirit to overcome our weaknesses, but it is a process, and even as we overcome some of them, there are others that still remain. We should learn to be happy about our progress instead of feeling guilty about how far we still have to go.

If we focus on our weaknesses we will continually feel discouraged, but if we focus on our progress it increases our joy.

Through my study of the word "weakness," I also learned that God encourages us to be long-suffering with the weak. We are told to bear with the failings of the weak, to endure, and carry one another's troublesome moral faults (Galatians 6:1–2). Surely, if God expects us to do that for one another, He is prepared to do it for us. God would never ask us to do something that He wasn't willing to do.

There is a wonderful story by Dan Clark called "Puppies for Sale" that gives us a beautiful picture of earthly love that mirrors God's love for us:

> *A little boy saw a sign on a store that said, "Puppies for Sale."*
> *He had always wanted a puppy so he went into the store and*
> *asked to see the puppies. Soon a beautiful Golden Retriever*
> *walked out of the backroom and five puppies followed her.*
> *One of them was lagging behind due to what appeared to be*
> *an injured leg. The boy asked how much the puppies were*
> *and was told thirty dollars. He only had two dollars and sev-*
> *enty cents, so he asked if could pay that now and then pay*
> *fifty cents each week until the puppy was paid for. While the*
> *owner was pondering the boy's proposal, he heard him say, "I*
> *want the one that is having trouble walking." The owner said,*
> *"Oh, I wouldn't even sell him; I will just give him away." The*
> *little boy said emphatically, "No, I will pay full price because*
> *he is worth just as much as the rest of them." The owner told*
> *the boy that he didn't recommend that puppy because since*
> *he was crippled he would never be able to run and play like*
> *other puppies and that he would not be very much fun. The*
> *boy insisted on having the crippled puppy and as the owner*
> *once again tried to change his mind, suddenly the boy pulled*
> *up his pant leg revealing a shriveled leg with a heavy metal*
> *brace on it. He said, "I want the crippled puppy because I will*
> *understand him and love him the way he is."*

Many people in the world feel that they are worthless and that nobody wants them because they have flaws, but Jesus understands and wants them! His strength is made perfect in our weakness (2 Corinthians 12:9). His love and total acceptance give us the courage to live with confidence in the midst of our imperfections.

You have permission to have weaknesses and not to have to constantly strive to attain something that is not attainable. You are probably feeling the same fear, and asking the same question that I did when I dared to believe this freeing truth: "If I think I am free to have weakness, won't it just invite me to sin more and more?" The answer is, no it won't. God's grace and love, and the freedom it offers, never entices us to sin more, but it does entice us to fall radically in love with Jesus. The more we realize that He loves us the way we are, the more we love Him, and that love for Him causes us to want to change for the right reason.

New Covenant Believers Living under the Old Covenant

God gave Israel the law through Moses. It was a system stating that if they would keep His law, then He would bless them. When they failed, sacrifices had to be made by them or the High Priest who stood in their place. These sacrifices atoned for their sins. They were given laws that told them the right thing to do, but they were not given any help in doing them. They had to try to be good, but they failed and had to make sacrifices to make up for their mistakes. This explanation, of course, is a very basic and simple one, but I hope it will serve my purpose in this portion of the book.

Under this old covenant, sin could be covered by these sacrifices, but never removed. The sense of guilt connected to sin was ever present. But the good news is that God has made a new covenant with man, and He ratified or sealed it in His own blood.

It is a better covenant and one that is far superior to the old. The old covenant was initiated with the blood of animals, but the new was initiated with the sinless blood of Jesus Christ.

Under the new covenant, Jesus fulfilled or kept all of the law of the old covenant and died in our place to pay for our sins and misdeeds. He took the punishment that we deserved, and promised that if we would believe in Him and all that He did for us, He would forever stand in our place, and our responsibility to keep the law would be met in Him. The problem that we have now is that many new covenant believers do believe in Jesus and accept Him as their Savior, but they still live under the old covenant by trying to keep the law in their own strength. The old covenant focused on what man could do, but the new covenant focuses on what God has done for us in Jesus Christ. (Read Hebrews 8 and 9 for more study in this area.)

The Law Cannot Perfect Us

For the Law never made anything perfect—but instead a better hope is introduced through which we [now] come close to God.

Hebrews 7:19

The law is perfect, but it cannot perfect us because we have no ability to keep it perfectly. We should avoid living under rules and regulations thinking that if we keep them perfectly God will be pleased. The sin principle in our flesh is actually incited and stirred up by the law.

Let's say that Mary attended a church that was very strict about regular church attendance. If she missed church an elder in the church called her to find out why she wasn't there. In addition they required their members to read the Bible through each year, and attend at least one of the church prayer meetings each week. They required all of the church members to serve in some capacity in the church. They had to work in the nursery, or do volunteer work of some kind. Now, all of these things may be good things in themselves, but the very fact that they were presented as rules to be followed would stir up something in Mary's flesh that would make her resent doing them. Mary would eventually not want to go to church, dread Bible reading and prayer and feel pressured by serving at church.

The more we are told that we cannot do something, the more we want to do it. If Mary thinks that she cannot miss church without being questioned, it will only make her not want to go. That, sadly, is human nature. If you repeatedly tell little Johnnie not to touch the glass table, he will become very interested in touching it even though he previously may not have even noticed it was there. Even if he is too frightened to touch it in front of you, he will certainly touch it when he believes you cannot see him do it. Your law against touching the glass table has actually given Johnnie an interest in doing it.

The law is good, but it cannot make us good. Only God can do that by giving us a new nature, a new heart and His Spirit. The law points out our weaknesses, but Jesus strengthens us in them. The law shows us our problem, but Jesus solves our problem!

God gave the law so we would eventually know that we needed a Savior. We can want to do what is right, but we have no ability to do it apart from God's continual help. It is interesting to realize that God gave the rules so we would find out that we couldn't keep them. The law is actually designed to bring us to the end of ourselves, or to the end of self-effort and works of the flesh. God's desire for us is that we learn to depend on Him in all things.

He does not want us to be self-reliant and He will not allow us to succeed as long as we are. The law is perfect, holy and righteous, and it shows us what sin is. The law was intended to lead us to Jesus, not to more and more struggling for perfection. It is intended to make us fully aware that we need God, and to make us learn to lean on Him. Jesus said, "Apart from Me you can do nothing" (John 15:5).

A legalistic approach to our relationship with God can actually steal every drop of life in us and leave us burned out and exhausted until we die to the law and begin to live for, in and through Christ.

> For I through the Law [under the operation of the curse of the Law] have [in Christ's death for me] myself died to the Law and all the Law's demands upon me, so that I may [henceforth] live to and for God.
>
> Galatians 2:19

Although I no longer strive for perfection, I do desire to do my best each day. Not to earn God's love or acceptance, but simply because I love Him. I encourage you to do the same thing.

When we love God we can never "not care" about improving our behavior, but we must fully understand that God's acceptance of us is never based on our behavior, but on our faith in Jesus. Our survey at the office revealed that many people simply wanted to know when they had done enough. Many of them, I am sure, had done their very best but still felt pressured to do more, and that is impossible. We can do our best, but we cannot offer God perfection, and we should not feel pressured to do so.

I heard a story about a student who turned a paper in to his professor and the professor wrote on the bottom of it, "Is this the best you can do?" and gave it back to him. Knowing it was not his best, the student did the paper again, and once again the professor gave it back to him with the same phrase at the bottom. This went on for about three rounds and finally when the professor asked if it was the best he could do, he thought seriously for a moment and answered, "Yes, I believe this is the best I can do." Then his professor said, "Good, now I will accept it." I think this story teaches us that all God wants is our best and He can work with that, even when our best is not perfect.

CHAPTER 4

The Anxiety and Anger of the Perfectionist

They say that nobody is perfect. Then they tell you prac-
tice makes perfect. I wish they'd make up their minds.
Winston Churchill

Sandra is a lovely young woman who has struggled with anger and perfectionism. Here is her story in her own words.

"For as long as I can remember I have worked desperately hard on what I call the 'treadmill of accomplishment' trying to be acceptable to myself. I have a strong tendency toward perfectionism and could not seem to rest unless everything on my list was accomplished. I would rarely allow myself to rest, or even if I was resting physically, I could not shut down mentally or emotionally. I didn't realize what was wrong but I felt as if I was working all the time and I lived with tremendous frustration.

"I desperately wanted to be at peace but couldn't seem to do it. My husband of twenty years is a person who loves peace and he watched me continually get frustrated with life and would pray for me that I would see what I was doing to myself. Yes, I was doing it to myself!

"I was anxious and angry most of the time, and even if I managed not to display it, I felt it inside. I wasn't angry at my family... just angry at myself for not being able to do it all! I felt like a failure at the end of each day because I set unrealistic and ridiculous (impossible to reach) goals for myself. When I saw that I was not going to get everything accomplished that I had planned to do I would go into a panic and try to work harder and faster. Of course my family could feel the frustration I lived with and if they needed my assistance with something while I was in panic mode it would make me even more panic-stricken, anxious and angry at myself. The more they needed, the more I felt like a failure.

"This had been the story of my life, and although I knew something about my life wasn't right, I couldn't put my finger on exactly what it was that was wrong. After all, what could be wrong with wanting to do everything right? There were even times when I felt like I hated my life, which was confusing to me because I have a wonderful husband and two beautiful girls and a lovely home. In addition to that I have known Jesus as my Savior since I was ten years old. So, why did I hate my life and feel unhappy? What I really hated was the fact that I felt like all I ever did was work. I really thought that my schedule and all that I had to do was my problem. I would frequently blurt out, 'I feel like all I ever do is work!'

"During the final months of 2011, I found myself crying out to God like never before saying, 'I just can't live like this anymore, God. I need serious help!' The New Year began and on January 2, during my devotional time with God, I asked Him if there was anything in particular that He wanted me to 'accomplish' in 2012. Well, He certainly did not want me to try to 'accomplish' something else, but He did have plenty to say to me that morning. I remember typing words into my journal so fast I could barely keep up. This is what I wrote:

My New Year's resolution this year is to think less and laugh more! I am way too mental about things and this year (2012)

I want to be more like Jesus. I have always wanted to be like Jesus, but it suddenly dawned on me that Jesus NEVER hurried and He was NOT stressed and anxious. He was NOT in a race with Himself, and never angry because He couldn't check everything off His list that day because He didn't have a list to start with. Jesus lived in close fellowship with His Father and spent His time helping and being good to people! I am getting off the accomplishment treadmill. I am done trying to get my worth and value out of being perfect so people will admire me, or even so I can admire myself. God thinks I am so special that He sent His Son Jesus to die on the cross for me, and He did it to save me from myself as well as from my sin. God loves me deeply. I receive His love, I consciously take it in, just like breathing.

"That day after typing everything into my journal, I prayed and asked God to forgive me for living like a fool in this area.

"I immediately noticed that I was responding differently in a variety of situations. Day after day, I watched carefully to make sure the change was real and not going to evaporate as quickly as it came. After a few weeks went by, I realized that on January 2 God gave me a revelation that was changing my life. One of the things I noticed was that I now looked at what I accomplished each day instead of what I didn't accomplish. I had turned from the negative to the positive! Having unfinished work didn't bother me anymore. The feeling of being a failure was completely gone. Previously I could rarely 'accomplish enough' to satisfy myself, but now, what I accomplished each day was good enough. My worth and value was no longer in what I accomplished, but in what Jesus had accomplished for me out of His deep love for me.

"Since then, there have been challenges along the way and times when I had to purposely hold on to my freedom. But when

I start to feel anxious, I stop and say, 'Sandra, you are okay even if this task doesn't get done right now.' Enjoyment and relaxation is something that I would not allow myself to enjoy before, but I am happy to say that it is a regular part of my life now!

"God has used many things to reinforce my newfound freedom, including my mom's book entitled *Do Yourself a Favor...Forgive.* I needed to realize that God was not mad at me and to forgive myself for being imperfect, and her book helped me do that.

"I feel as if I have been born again all over again, and it is amazing how much more I accomplish since God has delivered me from trying!"

Sandra is my daughter, and I am extremely happy for her because I watched her suffer most of her life with disappointment in herself because she could not be perfect. I remember her doing her homework as a little girl, crumpling up paper after paper and throwing them in the trashcan because she made a mistake and it wasn't perfect. She was anxious, frustrated and angry, but now she is peaceful, relaxed and happy. The same thing is available to everyone who needs it and is willing to believe the truth of God's Word. Declare boldly, "I don't have to be perfect, and I am not angry at myself." Now say, out loud **"God is not mad at me!"**

An Oversensitive Conscience

The Bible encourages us to maintain a conscience that is void of offense toward God and man. But if we have an oversensitive conscience, we will find that we feel guilty about many things that don't seem to bother other people. A symptom of perfectionism or a performance/acceptance mentality is anxiety. The tyranny of everything we think we ought to do and should have done or not done and the self-deprecation it creates produce an oversensitive conscience that is filled with anxiety, guilt and condemnation. I suffered with an oversensitive conscience because I desperately wanted to please God, but was also desperately afraid that I wasn't doing it. If my husband made a mistake, he got over it so quickly that it irritated me. It irritated me because when I made mistakes, I suffered for days agonizing over it, and I could not seem to shake the guilty feeling that my oversensitive conscience produced.

My earthly father had a knack for making me feel guilty even though I wasn't always sure what I'd done wrong. I assumed that his anger meant that I was guilty of something. After eighteen years of practice, while living at home with my parents, I had no experience with any way to live other than being "guilty." Now I know that I felt the wrong way about myself all of the time, and when God did deliver me through His Word and Holy Spirit, I actually went through a period when I felt guilty about my lack of guilt! I tell people, "I didn't feel right if I didn't feel wrong." That is deep bondage indeed, but fortunately I can say that I rarely feel guilty now, and if I am convicted of sin, I immediately repent, ask for and receive God's amazing forgiveness, and go on enjoying my life and fellowship with God. The same freedom that Sandra talked about, and that I am talking about, is available for you if you need it.

People who live with guilt often make a very deep commitment to God to do better and to try harder. They desperately want to rid themselves of the feeling of guilt, but I know from experience that merely "trying harder" is not the answer; in fact, it usually increases the problem. At a Christian conference or in a church service, it may sound plausible to make a deeper commitment and to think, "I am just going to try harder." But back in the real world, sooner or later we make mistakes and find once again that we are not perfect, and feel even more defeated than before.

When people try very hard and still experience failure, a cloud of doom often hangs over them and they can easily believe there is no hope, but in Christ there is always hope. The prophet Zechariah suggested that people be "prisoners of hope" and receive a double blessing for what they had lost (Zechariah 9:12). To be a prisoner means that we are locked up and unable to get away from a certain place or thing. Live your life locked up with hope and unable to get away from it and you will see amazing things happen. No matter what you have gone through or might be going through right now, you can hope (have faith) that God is working on your behalf right now and that you will see the results of His work in your life. You don't have to be a prisoner of your circumstances, but instead you can be a prisoner of hope.

There is freedom from an oversensitive conscience available, and it is found in studying God's Word. The more we study and get to know God personally, the more we know the truth, and it sets us free little by little. If you suffer with chronic guilt, please don't despair, but just keep studying the Word as God's personal message to you. It will drive the darkness out of your soul and you will have a healthy conscience that can receive conviction from the Holy Spirit, but not condemnation from the devil.

Lawmakers

The perfectionist can easily turn everything into a law or a rule that must be kept. When we make laws and try to keep them, we will always feel guilty when we don't. During what I call "my miserable years," I made a law of many things; one example was cleaning house. It had to be cleaned every day, and I mean everything dusted, mirrors shined, floors mopped and vacuumed, et cetera. I would not allow myself to go out with friends and have any enjoyment or relaxation until the house was cleaned. If I tried to enjoy myself, I felt guilty, not because I had really done anything wrong, but because I was living under laws I had made for myself. When the children came home after school and began messing the house up, I went into my fits, as I lovingly call them now. I nagged them all the time to pick things up. It was so bad that they really could not relax in my presence much of the time. Fortunately God changed me before much damage was done and I am happy to say that we all have great relationships now.

I felt better about myself when all of my surroundings were neat and tidy, but how we feel about ourselves should come from inside, not from outside. What kind of laws have you made for your own life? Anything that is a law becomes something that you are obligated to do, not something you enjoy doing. If prayer and Bible study is a law for you, then you probably dread it and find it hard to get to, but if you realize it is a privilege and not a law, you can enjoy it.

God does want us to discipline ourselves and to have good habits, but He doesn't want us to make laws for ourselves and other people. The law takes the life out of anything that we do. The law kills, but the Spirit makes alive (2 Corinthians 3:6). The only way a thing can be filled with life and joy is if we are led by the Holy Spirit to do it and if our motive for doing it is love for God and wanting to glorify Him.

You have made a law of a thing when you feel guilty if you miss doing it one time, even for a good reason. I exercise very regularly and to be honest, I hate to miss doing it, but I don't feel guilty if I do. I love to spend time with God, but I don't watch the clock while I do it so I can clock a certain prescribed time that I think I need to put in. I still like a clean house, but I no longer feel guilty if all my work is not finished at the end of the day because doing it is not a law to me. I will do it, but I will enjoy my life in the process. That is God's will for us!! He doesn't want us living stiff, wooden, rule-oriented lives that have no joy in them.

Here is an example that may help you understand further. Dave and I believe strongly that God wants us to help the poor, and we frequently help people who are begging on street corners, but we don't help everyone. It is not a law for us, but something that we are led by the Holy Spirit to do or not to do. I can remember feeling guilty if I didn't give something to each beggar that I saw, but in my heart I sensed that some of them were not poor, and that they were simply playing on people's emotions as a way to make money. When I gave to someone out of legalism, I didn't enjoy doing it, I merely felt obligated, but now that I have taken a step of faith and decided to trust myself enough to be led by the Holy Spirit in these areas and others, I no longer feel guilty if I don't give and I feel joy when I do. In the past week we have passed by three people begging on the side of the road, but we stopped and gave twenty dollars to only one. Why? We simply didn't have peace about the first two, but when we saw the third man, Dave and I both felt led to help him. These types of decisions are not made with the mind alone, but they are discerned in the spirit.

The apostle Paul gives us great insight in Romans chapter 7 about not making laws out of things, but instead learning to be led by the Holy Spirit.

> *But now we are discharged from the Law and have terminated*
> *all intercourse with it, having died to what once restrained*
> *and held us captive. So now we serve not under [obedience*

to] the old code of written regulations, but [under obedience to the promptings] of the Spirit in newness of life.

Romans 7:6

I think that we often make laws out of things because we are afraid to trust ourselves to be led by God's Spirit. I urge you to refuse to live a life legalistic and to trust God that He will teach you how to clearly be guided by Him in all things.

What Will People Think?

Perfectionists are very sensitive to what others think of them and they often try so hard to please so many people that they lose themselves. What I mean is that in an effort to please others, they rarely follow their own heart and do what is pleasing to them or to God.

Some people are addicted to approval. They cannot feel peaceful unless they believe that everyone is pleased with them, and that is something that is next to impossible to accomplish. We just can't please all the people all the time. The only way to avoid criticism is to do nothing, say nothing and be nothing, and that doesn't sound very inviting to me. The need to be popular can make you neurotic and steal your destiny. The apostle Paul said that if he had been trying to be popular with people, he would never have become an apostle of Jesus Christ (Galatians 1:10). Any time a person is a leader of other people, others will criticize

> *The only way to avoid criticism is to do nothing, say nothing and be nothing, and that doesn't sound very inviting to me. The need to be popular can make you neurotic and steal your destiny.*

him or her. As a leader, it is impossible for me to make one decision that will perfectly suit everyone, so I have to make my decisions based on what I believe God wants me to do, and not what people want me to do.

If Paul had an unbalanced need for approval, he could not have fulfilled his destiny. The Bible states that Jesus made Himself of no reputation (Philippians 2:7). He, too, knew the importance of not being overly concerned about other people's opinions.

We cannot always be God-pleasers and people-pleasers at the same time. If you are overly concerned about what people think of you, then you need to seriously consider what that is going to do to you long-term. People who are addicted to approval frequently get "burned out." They often attempt to do too much in order to meet all the expectations of the various people in their life. And it wears them out mentally, emotionally and physically. They are not good at saying "no," and once again the problem of perfectionism (in this case, a desire to please everyone perfectly) creates anxiety and anger. When we say "yes" to everyone, we feel used and pulled in too many directions, and then we get angry. But we are the only ones who can change our situation. We create many of our own problems, and we are the only ones that can solve them. Don't waste your time asking God to change something that He has already given you the power to change. Don't complain and live a silently angry life while at the same time continuing to do the very things that make you angry.

Although it is true that people should not pressure us to do everything they want us to do, it is equally true that we are the ones who have the responsibility not to allow ourselves to try to please them to the point that it causes us to feel pressured. Don't blame someone else for your failure to stand up for yourself.

People who step outside the box of what most people would

consider acceptable behavior are usually branded "rebellious." Are they really rebellious, or are they attempting to be true to their own selves? Was Peter stepping outside the box of what was normal when he stepped out of the boat and began to walk on water at Jesus' invitation to do so? The eleven disciples who remained in the boat probably thought Peter was very foolish. We often judge people who do what we would secretly like to do, but won't do for fear of what people will think.

You can buy friends and acceptance by letting people control you, but you will have to keep them the same way you obtained them. It becomes very draining after a time, and you will end up resenting them for the very thing you allowed them to do. I have come to believe that if I can never say no to a person in order to remain in relationship with him or her, then that is probably a relationship that I don't need.

Sometimes people we think are angry with us are not angry at all. It is our fears that give us that perception. Just as we can spend our life thinking that God is mad at us and He isn't, we can also imagine that other people don't approve of us, when in reality they may not even be thinking about us. Refuse to spend your life in fear of what people think, and begin to confront that fear. Get to the root of all your fears and you will probably find that most of them are unfounded and that they exist only in your imagination.

What Is the Answer to the Dilemma?

The pathway to God is not perfect performance. Some people in a crowd asked what they needed to do to please God, and the answer Jesus gave was, "Believe in the One Whom He has sent" (John 6:28–29). That is so simple that we miss it. We need to believe in Jesus? That's *it*? Surely God wants more out of us than that! More than anything, God wants us to trust Him and to believe His Word. You can get off the treadmill of trying to be perfect, because you cannot buy or earn God's love or favor, not even with a perfect performance. It simply is not for sale!

If we can't earn God's approval, then how can we get it? Receiving God's grace that is provided in Jesus is the answer to this problem. We must know that it is not anything we do, but God's amazing grace that invites us into a loving relationship with Him. Grace is a gift that cannot be purchased with our performance or anything else. It can only be received by faith. Grace is God's undeserved favor! It is His love, mercy and forgiveness available at no cost to us. Grace is also the power to change us and make us into what He wants us to be. There is no limit to God's grace and it is available to restore and lift us up any time we fail. You can be free today from the anger and anxiety that is produced by perfectionism by giving up your own works and fully trusting in the work that Jesus has done for us all. Remember, the work that God requires of you is that you believe in the One Whom He has sent (John 6:28–29).

Grace not only forgives us, it enables us to forgive those who have hurt us in life. Repressed anger about the way others have treated us is often the root of perfectionism and the anger and anxiety it causes. Forgiving our abusers or enemies is a major part of our own healing. While we are learning not to be angry with ourselves for our imperfections, let's also learn to give others the same grace that God gives us.

In his men's seminar, David Simmons, a former cornerback for the Dallas Cowboys, tells about his childhood home. His father, a military man, was extremely demanding, rarely saying a kind word, always punishing him with harsh criticism and insisting that he do better. The father had decided that he would never permit his son to feel any satisfaction from his accomplishments, reminding him there were always new goals ahead. When Dave was a little boy, his dad gave him a bicycle, unassembled, with the command that he put it together. After Dave struggled to the point of tears with the difficult instructions and many parts, his father said, "I knew you couldn't do it." Then he assembled it for him.

When Dave played football in high school, his father was unrelenting in his criticism. In the backyard after each game, his dad would go over every play and point out Dave's errors. "Most boys got butterflies in their stomach before the game; I got them afterward. Facing my father was more stressful than facing any opposing team." By the time he entered college, Dave hated his father and his harsh discipline. He chose to play football at the University of Georgia because its campus was farther from home than any other school that offered him a scholarship. After college, he became the second-round draft pick of the St. Louis Cardinals' professional football club. Joe Namath (who later signed with the New York Jets) was the club's first-round pick that year. "Excited, I telephoned my father to tell him the good news. He said, 'How does it feel to be second?'"

Despite the hateful feelings he had for his father, Dave began to build a bridge to his dad. Christ had come into his life during his college years, and it was God's love that made him turn to his father. During visits home he stimulated conversation with him and listened with interest to what his father had to say. He learned for the first time what his grandfather had been like—a tough lumberjack known for his quick temper. Once he destroyed a pickup truck with a sledgehammer because it wouldn't start, and he often beat his son. This new awareness affected Dave dramatically. "Knowing about my father's upbringing not only made me more sympathetic for him, but it helped me see that, under the circumstances, he might have done much worse. By the time he died, I can honestly say we were friends."

It is very helpful for us to remember that "hurting people hurt people." I don't think very many people wake up every day with the thought in mind of purposely seeing how much they can hurt everyone in their life, yet that is often exactly what they do. Why? Usually because they are hurting and have unresolved issues in their own life.

The healing of the damaged emotions that often cause perfectionism does take time, but no matter how long your journey takes, please remember that God loves you the same every step of the way. I saw a bumper sticker that read, *"CAUTION! God at work! Person in progress!"*

If you are afraid that you are not perfect, you don't need to be afraid anymore. I can assure you that you're not perfect so don't even think about it anymore. But I can also assure you of one more thing and that is, "God is not mad at you!"

CHAPTER 5

Father Issues

Although my father and my mother have forsaken me, yet the Lord will take me up [adopt me as His child].

Psalm 27:10

When we hear sermons about Father God from the pulpit, there is often a barrier between the message and the listeners. For many listeners (or readers), as soon as you use the word *father*, walls go up. Because of abusive fathers, negligent fathers or absentee fathers, our image of God as a father has become distorted and even painful.

If someone had an angry father, it is quite natural to view Father God as angry, too. That is why it's so important to deal with father issues in this book. I hope you are one of the blessed ones who had an awesome dad, but for many that is not the case.

I read that about 25 percent of American households are single-parent homes, and usually the parent is the mother. Out of the other 75 percent, many fathers are angry, abusive or rarely home. My father was angry and abusive, and I am sure that's the main reason I suffered so long thinking that God was angry, too. The atmosphere in the home I grew up in was very tense. It was everyone's goal in the house to keep Dad from getting mad, but it seemed that no matter what we did, he still found a reason to be angry. He was virtually impossible to please. I know now that he was angry with himself because of the sin in his life, but rather than face it, he deflected it onto other people. As long as he found something wrong with someone else, he didn't have to look at his own shortcomings.

My father sexually abused me for many years, got drunk every weekend and displayed violent rages in which he often ended up beating my mother. I don't even know how to properly describe the intense fear we lived in. I certainly never felt loved or cared for.

We Need to Feel Safe

One of our most urgent needs in life is to feel safe. But children who grow up with angry, absent or abusive fathers often don't feel safe. They have a feeling of impending doom or danger hanging over them most of the time. God wants us to feel safe with Him. He is a loving Father, kind, forgiving, generous, long-suffering, patient and faithful. But for those who have father issues, that truth is very hard to believe.

In his book *Holy Sweat*, Tim Hansel gives the perfect picture of a child who felt safe:

> *One day, while my son Zac and I were out in the country, climbing around in some cliffs, I heard a voice from above me yell, "Hey Dad! Catch me!" I turned around to see Zac joyfully jumping off a rock straight at me. He had jumped and then yelled "Hey Dad!" I became an instant circus act, catching him. We both fell to the ground. For a moment after I caught him I could hardly talk. When I found my voice again I gasped in exasperation: "Zac! Can you give me one good*

reason why you did that???" He responded with remarkable calmness: "Sure...because you're my Dad." His whole assurance was based in the fact that his father was trustworthy. He could live life to the hilt because his father could be trusted.

Zac's complete trust in his father enabled him to live freely and without fear. Sadly, many of us did not have that experience with our earthly fathers, but we can have it now with Father God. God is definitely not like people. If your earthly father was absent, you need to know that Father God is omnipresent, and that means He is everywhere all the time. You will never be anywhere that God is not with you.

If your earthly father was abusive or angry, your Heavenly Father wants to give you recompense for the way you were treated. He promises to give us a double reward for our former trouble if we will trust Him.

Instead of your [former] shame you shall have a twofold recompense; instead of dishonor and reproach [your people] shall rejoice in their portion. Therefore in their land they shall possess double [what they had forfeited]; everlasting joy shall be theirs.

Isaiah 61:7

The promise in this verse carried me through many dark and difficult days while I was working through the process of overcoming the way my father treated me, and it will help you, too, if you will take it as your own. Receive it as a direct promise from God to you. He is a God of justice. He loves to make wrong things right and He is waiting to do it for you.

God's Word has the power to heal our wounded souls. Consider these verses:

> *He sets on high those who are lowly, and those who mourn He lifts to safety.*
>
> Job 5:11

> *In peace I will both lie down and sleep, for You, Lord, alone make me dwell in safety and confident trust.*
>
> Psalm 4:8

> *And He led them on safely and in confident trust, so that they feared not; but the sea overwhelmed their enemies.*
>
> Psalm 78:53

> *Hold me up, that I may be safe and have regard for Your statutes continually!*
>
> Psalm 119:117

> *The fear of man brings a snare, but whoever leans on, trusts in, and puts his confidence in the Lord is safe and set on high.*
>
> Proverbs 29:25

> *[And indeed] the Lord will certainly deliver and draw me to Himself from every assault of evil He will preserve and bring me safe unto His heavenly kingdom. To Him be the glory forever and ever. Amen (so be it).*
>
> 2 Timothy 4:18

Considering, pondering and meditating on portions of Scripture like these will begin to build a trust for God in your heart.

You don't have to try to have it, just lean on God and His Word to do the work in you that needs to be done. His Word is powerful and it heals our brokenness.

The Character of God

When we say that a person's character is honest and trustworthy, we mean that person can always be counted on to tell the truth, act with the greatest honesty in all his or her dealings, and be trusted to keep his or her word. A character trait is something that is part of a person. It is not something the person does occasionally, but he or she does it all the time.

In order to trust Him completely, we must know the character of God. The thing that lies between knowing God and not knowing Him is seeking. God requires that we seek Him, that we have an intense desire to know Him. He states that if we seek Him, we will find Him. If you have no desire to seek and pursue God, then ask Him to give you one. Let's look at God's character.

God Is Good

God is good, without respect of persons. In other words, He is good to all, all the time. His goodness radiates from Him. If you were abused or abandoned in your childhood, you might be wondering why, if God is so good, He did not deliver you from those circumstances. I understand that question because I've asked it myself many times about my childhood. God has helped me over the years to understand that a parent has great authority over a child, and any wrong or sinful decisions they make do adversely affect their children, especially if there is no counteraction of a godly influence in the home.

For example, my husband's father was an alcoholic who was home most of the time physically, but in reality absent, since he spent most of his time in the basement drinking. His only function in the family was correcting the children when he didn't like what they were doing. Dave, however, seems to be unaffected by his father's behavior. As he and I have discussed this, we've realized that the godly influence of his mother and his own personal relationship with God acted as antidotes for the abusive behavior of his father.

If abuse exists in the home and there is no godly influence, more than likely a child will be adversely affected by the parent's behavior, but there is always hope of recovery. As soon as people are old enough to make their own choices, they can choose a relationship with God that can heal everything in their life

To be honest, very few people grow up without some kind of emotional pain that leaves scars. Even if our parents are good ones, we still must deal with the rest of the world and sooner or later we will run into someone who will hurt us. We must know how to receive healing from Jesus!

Not everything in our life is good, but God can work it out for good if we will trust Him. Joseph suffered much abuse at the hands of family members (his brothers) as a young boy, but later in life when he had an opportunity to get revenge on them, he said:

> As for you, you thought evil against me, but God meant it for good, to bring about that many people should be kept alive, as they are this day.
>
> Genesis 50:20

Joseph could have been bitter, but he searched for the good in his abusive situation and it helped him become a man of God who was used to bring help to millions in a time of famine. God didn't cause his abuse, but He certainly used it to train and empower Joseph for great things.

God's entire motive and purpose is to do good to everyone who will receive it from Him. The apostle James said there is no variation, not the slightest turning, in God's goodness (James 1:17). It is impossible for God not to be good, because it is His character. Don't ever think that God is like people, because His ways and thoughts are far above ours (Isaiah 55:8–9).

God Is Merciful

God is slow to anger and plenteous in mercy (Psalm 103:8). This aspect of God's character was difficult for me to receive because my father was such a hard, harsh man. He was quick to anger, and he always held grudges. If you got on his bad side, you stayed there for a long time.

Perhaps nothing you did was ever good enough for your father, but God is happy with any tiny effort we make to please Him. In His mercy, He overlooks what is wrong with our efforts and chooses to see what is right.

The Holy Spirit had to work with me a long time to finally get me to understand the freedom and joy of having a merciful heavenly Father who actually *wants* to forgive our transgressions. It is impossible to deserve mercy, and that is why it is such a waste of time to try to pay for our mistakes with good works or guilt. We don't deserve mercy, but God gives it freely!

Mercy overrides the rules. You may have grown up in a home that had lots of rules and if you broke any of them, you got into trouble. Although God does intend for us to keep His commands, He understands our nature and is also ready to extend mercy to anyone who will ask for and receive it.

*But I have trusted, leaned on, and been confident in Your
mercy and loving-kindness; my heart shall rejoice and be in
high spirits in Your salvation.*

Psalm 13:5

Although we don't experience a lot of mercy being extended
to us from people in the world, God does extend it at all times.
When we learn to receive mercy, then we will also be able to
give it to others and that is something that most people seriously
need. Mercy delivers us from the fear of punishment, or of being
rejected. When I broke one of my father's rules, I knew he would
shut me out of his fellowship, make me feel isolated and find a
way to punish me. I am thankful to say that I have never experienced that with my heavenly Father since I have come to truly
know His character.

God Is Faithful

Your earthly father may have walked away from you, leaving you
deeply hurt by his unfaithfulness and disloyalty. You may have
even thought that it was your fault that he left, even though that
was not true. You may have thought your dad left because you
were bad, so it would be easy to think that if you are bad, God
will leave you, too. But I can assure you that God is in your life to
stay.

I have experienced the unfaithfulness of people many times in
my life, but at the same time, I have experienced the faithfulness
of God. Indeed, God is not like people!

God promises that He will never leave you nor forsake you, but
will be with you until the very end (Matthew 28:20).

He is with you in your times of need and He is planning to pro-

vide for all your needs (Hebrews 13:5). God is with you when you
are going through trials and He is planning your breakthrough (1
Corinthians 10:13). When all others forsake you, God will stand
by you (2 Timothy 4:16–17).

Look at the apostle Paul's attitude:

> *Alexander the coppersmith did me great wrongs. The Lord*
> *will pay him back for his actions.*
>
> 2 Timothy 4:14

The apostle Paul trusted that God would take care of the entire
situation and bring recompense, or a reward, to him for the pain
he had endured. But keep in mind that we only see that reward
when we choose to have a godly attitude in our pain.

> *At my first trial no one acted in my defense [as my advocate]*
> *or took my part or [even] stood with me, but all forsook me.*
> *May it not be charged against them!*
> *But the Lord stood by me and strengthened me.*
>
> 2 Timothy 4:16–17

Paul's friends should have stood by him when he needed
them, but they didn't. And he actually asked God not to hold
their unfaithfulness against them. Why? I think it was because
he understood the weakness of man's nature. He didn't focus on
what people didn't do for him, but he focused on the fact that
although all others left him, the Lord stood by him. His heavenly
Father was faithful. We have no promise from God that people
will always be faithful, but we do have His promise that He will
be faithful at all times. People may shift and change, but God is
unchanging.

God Cannot Lie

People may lie to us. My father lied to me. He promised me things and then refused to do what he had promised when the time came. I remember one instance when he had told me that I could go to the movies with some kids from school on Friday night, and then when Friday came, for no reason at all, he said I couldn't go, and I was devastated. With my father, things like this happened all the time, but God cannot lie. It is impossible for His Word to fail, and we can step out onto it with certainty (Hebrews 6:17–19).

> *Heaven and earth will perish and pass away, but My words will not perish or pass away.*
>
> Mark 13:31

Perhaps you feel that God did let you down at some time in your life, or that one of His promises did not come true for you. If so, I urge you to realize that God doesn't always work within our time frame or in the ways that we would choose, but if you continue to trust Him, you will see the goodness of God in your life. Trust God at all times, and never give up. This is one of the ways that we can be faithful to God, as He is to us.

No matter how unfaithful your father or others may have been to you, I urge you not to let it ruin your life. There is no better day than today for a fresh start. Make a decision to believe that your heavenly Father is faithful and don't ever give up.

God Is Faithful to Forgive

God is always faithful to forgive our sins just as He promised He would. Sometimes people won't forgive us, but God always forgives sin and then forgets it. It is also good to know that there is no limit to God's forgiveness. People often have limits to what they are willing to forgive or how often they are willing to do it, but God's forgiveness never runs out. People may say they forgive us, but then remind us of what we did that hurt them, but God never reminds us of our past sins, because He has forgotten them (Hebrews 10:17). When we are reminded of past sins it is not God bringing them to our remembrance, but it is Satan, the Accuser of God's people.

God's faithfulness surrounds Him. It is part of His character and we can always count on Him to be with us and do all that He has promised to do.

God Is Love

My father told me all the time that he loved me, but the kind of love he had was sick and immoral. My mother told me that she loved me, but she didn't protect me from my father's abuse even though she knew about it. My first husband told me that he loved me but he was unfaithful many times. The list could go on, but I am sure you have a list of your own and that you probably relate to what I am saying. My point is that the words, "I love you," to many are mere words with no meaning.

However, when God says that He loves us, He means it in every way that is important and vital to us. His love always moves Him to action on our behalf, and true love can only be known by the actions that it prompts (1 John 3:16–18). You will see and experience the love of God being manifested in your life if you put your faith in it. Let me ask you if you have decided to believe that God loves you unconditionally and that He has a good plan for your life. I pray that you have and that you will begin to expect to see it manifested in your life. I encourage you to say several times each day out loud, "God loves me unconditionally and something good is going to happen to me today." By doing this you are verbally agreeing with God's Word, and helping to renew your own thinking.

The love of God (agape) seeks the welfare of all and works no ill toward any. It seeks an opportunity to do good to all men. The God kind of love is the love of a perfect being toward entirely unworthy objects (us). It produces a love in us for God, and a desire to help others seek the same.

God's Word states that He loves us because He wants to, and it is His kind intent. God loves because He must—it is who He is. God is love!

Learning to receive the unconditional love of God is the foundation for the rest of our relationship with God. How can we trust people if we are not sure that they love us? How can we expect them to be good or faithful? We cannot! We must have the "Does God love me?" question settled forever. Yes and a thousand times yes—GOD LOVES YOU!

Once again I would encourage you to go to God's Word and let it convince you.

> Even as [in His love] He chose us [actually picked us out for Himself as His own] in Christ before the foundation of the world, that we should be holy (consecrated and set apart for Him) and blameless in His sight, even above reproach, before Him in love.
>
> Ephesians 1:4

Reading this verse once won't convince you that God loves you if you doubt that He does, but if you really begin to seriously think about what it says, the power of it will seep into your soul and bring a revelation of His love that will be life-changing.

God decided to love us before we even arrived on planet earth. The only thing that stands between us and God's love is our being willing to believe Him and receive it.

In God's love He chooses to see us as blameless and above reproach (blame), and He sets us apart for Himself and makes us His own possession.

The apostle Paul urges us to let nothing separate us from the love of God, for it is indeed the most empowering force in the world.

There are of course many other wonderful aspects of God's character, but I mentioned the ones in this chapter as an aid to help my readers settle the father issues in their life once and for all. God is far above people, and His ways are perfect. Trust Him and let His love heal you.

A staff member at Joyce Meyer Ministries recounts:

> I gave my life to Christ in 1984, however I have been through two failed marriages and lots of disappointments in my life. Although I believed in God and loved Jesus, I did not believe that God loved me personally. All through grade school and high school I was ridiculed and made fun of. My first husband ran away with a seventeen-year-old girl after just four years of marriage. Through my last marriage of twenty-three years, I had become extremely codependent. When that ended, I was hurt and angry and again I was rejected. I believed I was a failure. My self-worth was at its lowest low. I had been told most of my life that I was fat and ugly, and I felt unlovable. I was used by men and had a great distrust of them, especially any man that was in authority over me.
>
> It sounds so easy, "Just accept this gift of God's love." But I felt unlovable. I would look in the mirror and see an

ugly person in the reflection; in my mind I would say, "Who could love this?" Years of rejection and hurt had caused me to believe these lies. Keep in mind that I was serving God and going to church this whole time, but I still believed I was unlovable.

In 2010 I was hired at the ministry and in the fall of that same year I started attending the ministry's inner-city outreach church, the St. Louis Dream Center. On Tuesday nights they provided a class called Experiencing the Father's Embrace. I yearned to understand God's love for me but knew the journey would be painful as I relived my past hurts in order to understand why I could not grasp this concept. Many old wounds were opened and exposed. I had to forgive in order to move on with my life. The person teaching our class said, "I challenge you to stand in front of the mirror and say, 'God loves me,' not just once but five to ten times a day or every time you walk by a mirror." I had to stop, look directly into my own eyes and say it. I reluctantly followed her instructions. It took several months but one day I began to believe it. I truly believed that God loved me! Me! Wow! I am loved!

CHAPTER 6

The Pain of Rejection

He who hears and heeds you [disciples] hears and heeds
Me; and he who slights and rejects you slights and rejects
Me; and he who slights and rejects Me slights and rejects
Him who sent Me.

Luke 10:16

You can escape the bondage and pain of rejection and experience the freedom of God's acceptance. None of us experiences acceptance from everyone in our life, and although rejection hurts, we are able to look at it realistically and not be adversely affected by it, but many of us experience a type of rejection that damages our souls. It is a pain so deep that it makes us reject and dislike ourselves. We believe that we are flawed if people reject us and therefore we erroneously decide that we are worthless. That mentality is very harmful to us because God created us for love and acceptance and nothing else will ever satisfy us. Until we have it, we will hunger for it, and may sadly look for it in all the wrong places.

Interestingly, many of the world's most successful people and many world leaders are people who have a **root of rejection** in their life. That means they have experienced feelings of rejection that are so deep it has affected their entire manner of thinking, feeling and behaving throughout their lives. The rejection they feel is at the base of all their decisions and it colors their entire life. They are so determined to prove they are worth some-thing that they try harder than others and do eventually succeed, at least in business, ministry or politics. But quite often, though not always, they are *not* successful at being fully formed, healthy human beings. "Who" they are is based on what they "do," and if they ever stop doing it, they are once again worthless in their own estimation. We must all beware of letting our value rest in what we do, because no matter what it is that we do, the day will probably come when we won't do it any longer.

> We must all beware of letting our value rest in what we do, because no matter what it is that we do, the day will probably come when we won't do it any longer.

Not everyone with a root of rejection is successful in climbing to the top of their profession; in fact, they may go to the opposite extreme and withdraw from life in general. They decide that if they never try anything, then they can't be rejected for not suc-ceeding. One thing is for sure, however we respond to the dam-age done by severe rejection, it is always in a way that is out of balance. We either work too hard, or we don't do anything at all. We either have no friends, or we try to have more friends than anyone in order to prove to ourselves that we are acceptable. We buy nothing for ourselves because we don't think we deserve it, or we make the pursuit of things our main goal in life in order to feel complete.

Our real success and value in life is not found in climbing what the world calls the ladder of success. It is not in a job promotion, a bigger house, a better-looking car, or being in the right social circles. True success is knowing God and the power of His resur-rection. To know that He loves you unconditionally and that you are made acceptable in Jesus, the Beloved Son of God Who died for you to pay for your sins. True success is being the best you can be, but never having to be better than someone else to prove that you are valuable.

A book called *The Hidden Price of Greatness* relates the stories of many great men and women of God who were used by Him in mighty ways. We can learn some powerful truths by looking at the background of these individuals. The book explains how childhood suffering often sets the stage for a life of struggle. For example, David Brainerd's father died when David was eight years old. His mother died when he was fourteen. And even though he inherited a sizable estate, he lost the parental love and affection that is so essential to a child's happiness and security.

Brainerd, like many abandoned, rejected, neglected and abused children, felt an unusual burden of guilt—almost as if he had been responsible for his parents' deaths. The author relates that the Holy Spirit repeatedly tried to make real to David Brainerd that his sufficiency was in Christ. Apparently he would get some insight and try to practice it for a little while, but would go right back into the "works and suffering" mentality as he tried to be perfect in himself.

Brainerd died at the age of twenty-nine. Although he had a powerful ministry that is still spoken of today, he had become an invalid—too ill to preach, teach or pray. The young man had utterly exhausted himself, trying to serve God perfectly.

I certainly understand this, because I've experienced my own version of Brainerd's dilemma. Fortunately, I learned the truth in time to stop me from continuing to abuse myself in my effort to be acceptable to God. I did suffer for a long time, even though the Holy Spirit was working in me and revealing truth to me. I would enter God's rest for periods of time, and then the devil would attack me again. When Satan knows where we are vulnerable, he will attack there again and again to see if there is any remaining weakness he can play on. Eventually I was strong enough in my faith to rest assured of God's love and acceptance apart from any works I did. I became free, and I still enjoy that freedom today.

Jesus did not enjoy the acceptance or approval of most people while He was on earth. He was despised and rejected by men! But he knew his heavenly Father loved Him. He knew who He was and it gave Him confidence.

Everything that Jesus endured and suffered was for our sake. He went through rejection, so when we face it, we too can go through and not be damaged by it, or if we have already been damaged, then we can completely recover. Jesus never promised us that everyone would accept and approve of us; as a matter of fact, He told us just the opposite. He said that if we choose to follow Him, we will be persecuted for righteousness' sake. If we make it through childhood without any traumatic experience of rejection, we may well experience some from friends and family if we decide to fully follow Jesus. People don't mind so much if we are merely religious and occasionally go to church; however, if we get serious and actually allow Christ to change us, it often bothers people.

When I answered the call of God to teach His Word, I experienced massive rejection from many people, and some of them were the ones that I loved the most and had previously thought loved me, too. It is amazing how people's commitment to us changes when we are no longer doing what they want us to do. That period of my life was extremely painful to me, especially since I already had a root of rejection in my life from my childhood.

Press Through the Pain

Jimmy was four years old and very excited about being on the soccer team. His mom took him to all the practices and now it was time for him to play his first game, but it turned out horribly!

Jimmy was doing fine and having lots of fun until about halfway through the game. A big kid came up to him and socked him very hard in the stomach! Jimmy doubled up in pain and fell to the ground crying. The kid said something to him and he ran to the sideline. When his mom got him quieted down and asked what was wrong, he said, "That big boy punched me in the stomach, and he told me, 'You're no good. You'll never learn how to play soccer. You're not doing anything right! You get off this field and don't come back here and try to play with us anymore!'" When they got home Jimmy said, "I'm never going back there again!"

This is a classic example of what happens to millions of people. Even at that young age, Jimmy experienced the pain of rejection. Experiences like this ruin many people's lives and prevent them from being the person God wants them to be, unless they learn how to press through the pain.

I recall an instance in my childhood that devastated me. I was about six years old, and my class at school was having a Halloween party. Lots of the girls were princesses, Cinderella or a ballerina, and their costumes were beautiful. My parents didn't want to spend much money on getting me an outfit and my mom didn't sew, so she bought me a rubber wolf mask. It was extremely ugly, and I wore it with my regular clothes. I was hurt that my parents didn't want me to look beautiful, too, and they were not willing to spend a little bit of money on a costume for me. I recall hiding in the corner of the schoolyard at recess, desperately hoping that nobody would notice how ugly I was. It must have had a huge impact on me, because I can still see it today very plainly. Although it was a seemingly minor occurrence, at the age of six it was extremely painful to me.

Childhood traumas like these have a way of lingering in our minds; we often wince at the memory. You may be remembering a similar event that happened to you and are aware that it has held you back in life. This may sound like an exaggeration, but children are like tender saplings; even a small wind can break their little limbs. The good news is that it's not too late! You can shake off the effects of those unfortunate experiences and go on to do great things. Whether the pain of rejection comes from something major or minor, it is a very real pain, and unless it is dealt with it can have lasting effects.

I am very grateful that God gave me the grace to press through the pain of the rejection I experienced and to follow Him. I can't imagine what I would be doing today if I had not, but I do know that I would probably be living in bondage and pain.

The devil uses the pain of rejection to try to prevent us from living the life God intends for us to live. I am sure the world is filled with people who are dissatisfied and unfulfilled. They let the fear of man's rejection determine their destiny, instead of following their own heart, and in an effort to keep other people happy, they have ended up unhappy themselves. I urge you not to do this, or if you already have, then begin rectifying it. As believers in Christ, we have the privilege of being led by the Holy Spirit, and He will always lead us to the perfect place if we let Him. Of course Satan will try to hinder us, just as he tried to hinder Jesus from following God's will for Him.

Jesus was rejected and despised by many individuals and groups, the religious leaders of that time and even his brothers.

Peter denied Him, and Judas betrayed Him, and yet He pressed through the pain and obeyed His heavenly Father.

Satan plants "seeds" of rejection in us, hoping they will grow into huge plants in our lives that will bear poisonous fruit. But, if we remember that God never rejects us and that His will for us is that we be loved and accepted, we can realize that rejection is an attack from the devil and we can refuse to let it have an adverse affect on us. Knowing how valuable you are to God, and that He has an amazing plan for your life, will enable you to endure the pain of rejection for the joy of what lies on the other side of it.

Each time you experience rejection, remind yourself that God loves you; that when people reject you, it doesn't mean something is wrong with you. While we need to have compassion for other people's problems, we can't let them project their problems onto us. My father rejected me as a daughter and sexually abused me, and for years I believed that it was because something was wrong with me. My father was harsh and mean, hateful and controlling. He used people to get what he wanted, with no concern for how his actions affected them. I eventually realized that what he did to me was not my fault, but I did suffer with the pain of rejection for many years.

My first husband rejected me for another woman while I was pregnant with his child, and it compounded my belief that I was useless, worthless and no good. Each thing that happened to me served to convince me more and more that I was deeply flawed and unlovable. Finally I realized that my first husband had the problem, not me. He was the one who was unfaithful, not me. He went to prison because he was a thief, not me. He lied, would not work, used people and added no value to anyone. But during the time that he was rejecting me, I could not see past my pain, and it was easy for Satan to deceive me and blame me for the problems we had.

If you are experiencing the pain of rejection right now in your life, stop and seriously think about the person who is rejecting you. I am sure if you look at their behavior and their actions, not only toward you but toward other people as well, you will realize that they have the problem, not you. I was recently answering questions on a radio call-in show and a woman called in to say, "My husband is addicted to pornography, and a year ago he told me that I look disgusting compared to the women he looks at online or in magazines, and that I could never make him feel the way they do." She was devastated by his statement and seemed to be unable to get beyond it, so she was asking for advice. I told her that she had to realize that he had a problem and not to let him blame it on her. Hurting people hurt people! Something was wrong inside him that made him want to do what he was doing, and his behavior was sinful. I told her to pray for him, and to let him know that he could not make her feel bad about herself, because she knew that God loved her.

Don't let someone else's bad behavior toward you make you feel bad about yourself. I realize that it is easier said than done, because our emotions and feelings get involved and emotional pain is actually one of the worst kinds of pain we experience. We can take a pain pill to get rid of physical pain, but no pills are available for emotional pain. That is why we must recognize it for what it is and know that if we don't feed it by giving in to it, it will eventually fade and go away. You can't help feeling it, but you don't have to let it determine your actions. You can learn to manage your emotions and not let them manage you. You can learn to live beyond your feelings! Press through the pain and live your life!

Don't Reject Yourself

The devil's long-term goal is that we ultimately reject ourselves and live a life of misery. The devil is against us and he wants us to be against us, too. Fortunately, God is for us, and when we learn how to agree with God and what He says about us in His Word, the devil loses out entirely and his plan does not succeed.

I can't even count all the times and ways in my life that I have experienced deeply painful rejection, but I am happy to say that through God's help and healing power, I like myself! We should all have a healthy love and respect for ourselves. I like to say, "Don't be in love with yourself, but do love yourself." If Jesus loved you enough to die for you, you should never demean or reject yourself.

God's desire is that we become trees of righteousness bearing good fruit (Isaiah 61:3). However, if we reject ourselves, our fruit will be fear, depression, negativism, lack of self-confidence, anger, hostility and self-pity. And that is just the beginning of all the bad fruit we will have. We will also be confused and totally miserable. It is impossible to be happy if you hate and despise or reject yourself.

No matter how many other people love you, if you don't love yourself, you will still feel lonely.

> No matter how many other people love you, if you don't love yourself, you will still feel lonely.

Causes and Results of Rejection

You may feel as if you have always been unhappy and you just don't know what is wrong. I knew a woman like that. She was a fine Christian woman who had a lovely family and home, but she could not seem to get beyond the feeling that something was missing inside her. She was tormented with feelings of insecurity and being unloved. She eventually discovered that she had been adopted, that her birth mother didn't want her and she had been left on the doorstep of a hospital.

There are many things that can open the door for a spirit of rejection to fill our souls and being to rule our lives. It's good for us to know the root causes of the rejection we feel because the truth sets us free. Sometimes the sheer act of understanding will help us to deal with an issue effectively.

Here are some of the things that may cause a person to feel rejected. Look them over and ask yourself if any of them relate to you or someone you know.

Unwanted conception

A mother who contemplated or attempted abortion

A child born of the wrong sex, in the parents' eyes (for example, they wanted a boy and got a girl)

Parents disappointed with a child who is born with physical or mental disabilities

Comparison to another sibling

Adoption

Death of one or both parents

Abuse, including physical, verbal, sexual, emotional and the withholding of affection

A parent with mental illness (the child may feel abandoned)

Divorce

Peer rejection

Turmoil within the home

Rejection in marriage, or an unfaithful spouse

Did you get stuck in the pain of an event that you cannot go back and undo? If so, don't stay there. Let what is behind remain behind, and let it make you better rather than bitter.

Below is a list of some of the behaviors that are fruits of rejection and often plague people who feel that they were not loved and accepted during their formative years. Do any of them feel familiar?

Anger—People who have been hurt feel anger over what they have unjustly suffered. The natural tendency is to feel that someone owes us.

Being judgmental—When people feel bad about themselves, they frequently find fault in others to deflect their own guilt.

Bitterness—Everything about our life can become bitter when we are functioning from a root of rejection.

Competition—A person who feels insecure may compete with others, always trying to be better than them, or at the very least just as good.

Defensiveness—Even though we may feel worthless, we will often still defend ourselves if anything is said that may add to our present feelings of rejection.

Disrespect—If we are distrusting and suspicious, we will tend to also disrespect people.

Distrust—If we feel unloved, we will even distrust people who say they love us. We will be suspicious and expect everyone to hurt us eventually.

Escapism, including drugs, alcohol and being excessive in things like shopping, work, sleeping, overeating and television—When our pain is extreme, we often find ways to avoid it.

Fear of all types—Rejection can cause phobias of all kinds. A person may become paralyzed with fear and let it rule their life.

Guilt—We may feel that the rejection we experienced is our fault and therefore live with a vague sense of guilt.

Hardness—People may develop a hardness in their soul that they think will protect them from further pain, but it ends up hurting other people in the same ways they are trying to avoid being hurt.

Hopelessness—We may live with a feeling that nothing good will ever happen to us, so why bother even thinking that it might.

Inferiority—We may feel that we are not as good as other people and fall into the trap of comparing ourselves to them.

Jealousy—Not knowing our value drives us to want what other people have in order to make us feel that we are equal with them. We can easily resent the blessings of others if we have a root of rejection.

Perfectionism—We may strive for perfection, thinking that then no one will be able to find any fault with us.

Poor self-image—We may view ourselves as failures in general and feel bad about ourselves in every way.

Poverty—If we feel worthless, we may feel we are not deserving of anything, and we therefore will not work in order to have anything.

Rebellion—When we have been hurt, especially if someone in authority has hurt us, we may fear being hurt again and rebel against all authority.

The good news is that each of these wrong behavior patterns finds its solution in God's Word. I can safely say that I manifested all of these behaviors at one time or another in my life, but through studying and believing God's Word, I have also experienced freedom from all of them.

If you need help in these areas, please believe me when I say that Jesus is your answer. You don't have to spend your life suffering over the way other people have treated you or because of things that have happened to you. God has provided a way out and a place of safety for you. God loves you; He will never reject you and He is not mad at you!

CHAPTER 7

Learning to See Clearly

[For I always pray to] the God of our Lord Jesus Christ, the Father of glory, that He may grant you a spirit of wisdom and revelation [of insight into mysteries and secrets] in the [deep and intimate] knowledge of Him.

Ephesians 1:17

I have dry eyes and frequently have to put thick eye drops in my eyes for moisture. After I use them, my vision is blurry for a while and I can't see clearly. I can see, but everything I see is distorted. That is the way we see the world and ourselves when we are operating out of a root of rejection and feelings of worthlessness. Our perception of reality is blurred, and we misjudge many things. We may imagine that someone is ignoring us when the truth is that they didn't even see us.

I vividly recall a woman who attended some of my weekly Bible studies in the 1980s. A friend informed me that the lady, whom we will call Jane (not her real name), was deeply hurt because I never talked to her. I was shocked when I heard it because I didn't remember seeing the lady. I knew her and knew she attended my teaching sessions, but so did five hundred other women, and I could not possibly personally speak with every one of them.

I prayed about this situation because it was not my desire to hurt anyone, and I felt that God showed me that He purposely didn't let me notice her, because she wanted attention from me for the wrong reason. She was very insecure and wanted the attention to make her feel better about herself. God wanted her to come to Him to have her needs met. He wanted her to find her value in His love for her. I am happy to say that Jane ended up receiving healing from God and worked on my staff for twenty years. Even then, I still did not see her very often because of the area she worked in, but it didn't matter to her because she no longer *needed* me to pay attention to her.

I would like to say that everyone who is insecure receives this type of healing and goes on to fulfill his or her destiny; sadly, that is not the case. But it can be if he or she will learn to see clearly.

The way we view everything in life is determined by our inner thought life. We see through our own thoughts, and if those thoughts are in error, then we see things in a wrong way.

For example, many married couples have difficulty communicating. They begin to discuss an issue, and before long they find themselves angry and arguing about things that have nothing at all to do with the thing they intended to discuss. They get lost in a maze of accusation and frustration, and the conversation ends with one or the other of them throwing their hands up in the air in exasperation and saying, "I just cannot talk to you about anything!"

Does that sound familiar? It does to me, because Dave and I went through it countless times until I learned that my old wounds of rejection were affecting my perception. I wasn't seeing clearly and I believed all sorts of things that just were not true. For example, if Dave didn't agree with me on all points, I received his disagreement as a rejection of me as a person, rather than a rejection of my opinion. If he didn't agree with me on everything (and I do mean everything), then I felt wounded and unloved.

Those feelings led me to blame him for the way I felt and then attempt to manipulate him into agreeing with me.

I recall getting so confused during those times. It frustrated me that we couldn't seem to talk about things, but I honestly did not know what was wrong! I assumed it was Dave being stubborn, but eventually I found out that the root of rejection in my life was still coloring all my conversations, and especially confrontation.

We must let God remove the wrong perceptions that color our thinking and replace them with right, godly perceptions about ourselves and others. This is done as our mind is renewed through studying God's Word.

If we are not thinking clearly, we might think we are not capable of doing something that in reality we could do very well if we would only step out and try. We might view ourselves as a failure waiting to happen because of things that have been said to us during our life, but what does God say? He says that we can do all things through Him, and that we need not fear man or failure. We can live boldly, and we can try things to find out if we can do them or not. How will you ever know what you are good at if you are so afraid of failure that you never try to do anything?

We make every effort to not experience the pain of rejection, and this often causes us to let our feelings dictate our behavior and choices. We need to live beyond our feelings. The book of Proverbs encourages us repeatedly to get skillful and godly wisdom, to get understanding (comprehension and discernment). This means we are to learn to think clearly, or to learn to think with the mind of the spirit, instead of the mind of the flesh.

When we think naturally, according to our own views and feelings, we are thinking with the mind of the flesh. God's Word states that this is sense and reason without the Holy Spirit, and that it brings us death and all the miseries that arise from sin (Romans 8:6). This morning I noticed that I felt tense, and I wasn't relaxed and didn't know why. Instead of just trying to press through the day and be confused all day about what was wrong with me, I stopped and asked God for understanding and discernment. I knew that was not the way God wants me to feel, so what was behind it? I quickly realized that I was vaguely worrying about something that someone I love was doing that I thought was not a good choice. It was something I could not control and in reality was none of my business. My only option was to pray and trust God to reveal truth to the person if he was making a mistake in his decision.

Taking the time to think more clearly enabled me to press past my upset and go ahead and enjoy my day. It enabled me to think with the mind of the Holy Spirit. I invited Him into my thinking when I asked for wisdom and discernment. He helped me see the situation clearly. I encourage you to stop any time you feel pressure, upset, frustration or tension and ask God to show you why you feel that way. You will be able to see more clearly and it will help you move past the problem.

I urge you to pray daily for wisdom to flow through you, and for deep discernment and understanding. Ask God for truth in every situation. Don't be afraid to face truth if you are the one that is deceived. Being free is much more important than being right. It was a bit difficult for me to face the reality that most of the arguments Dave and I had were the result of my old wounds. It was even more difficult to apologize and tell him that I knew it was mostly my fault, but swallowing my pride was a small price to pay for freedom.

> Being free is much more important than being right.

If you still react to people and situations out of old wounds of rejection, abandonment or abuse, you can be free. Not only will you enjoy your freedom, but the other people in your life will enjoy it also. I know it was very difficult for Dave all the years I wasn't thinking clearly and reacted to everything emotionally, instead of with the mind of the Spirit. Your willingness to change will be a blessing to many people.

Rejection and Confrontation

People who devalue themselves and have a root of rejection don't handle confrontation or any kind of correction very well. They usually become defensive and try to convince the people confronting them that they are wrong in their assessment of them.

No one enjoys being told they are wrong about something and that they need to change, but a secure individual can handle it much better than an insecure one. Accepting God's love and approval and being rooted in it will help us receive confrontation with a good attitude. The person confronting us may or may not be right, but at least we can listen without becoming angry.

If you can handle knowing that you are not perfect, it won't upset you when other people tell you that you are not. Seminary professor and author Steve Brown has learned what he calls the Bingo Retort. After hearing him speak at a seminar, a man came to him offering several corrections. He began his confrontation with, "What you said today grieved my heart. I think you are arrogant, rude and prideful," and Steve replied, "Bingo, you have read me well; if you had known me several years ago, you would have been even more grieved." Steve is not afraid to be challenged, because he already knows he is not perfect. He says that when people tell him he is wrong about something, he says, "Bingo, I am wrong at least 50 percent of the time." Or, if someone tells him he is selfish, he says, "Bingo, my mother told me the same thing, and my wife knows it, too."

Just think how much anger and emotional pain this saves him. If someone rejects us because we are not perfect, it won't bother us if we are already aware that we are not perfect and have no problem with it. It is not really what people say and do to us that makes us miserable, but how we respond. If we have a healthy attitude toward ourselves, we won't be bothered by what others think.

Yesterday, I went to an appointment I had and a woman recognized me. She asked if she could hug me and while doing so said, "I don't care what people say about you; I think you are wonderful!" She could have just said, "I hear a lot of people say bad things about you." I admit that I felt a little pinch of pain when she said it, but I quickly shook it off and went on to have a great day. I actually laughed with others about what she said several times. I thought it was ironic in light of the fact that I was working the day before this on the chapters in the book on rejection.

I also thought about how I handled the situation compared to how I would have handled it twenty years ago. Back when I still had a root of rejection I would have wanted to know who said bad things and exactly what they said. Then I would have defended myself and probably been upset for days over the thought that people are saying bad things about me. I am so glad I didn't have to wear myself out emotionally with being upset over what some people think. I choose to believe that the people who like me outnumber the ones who don't, so I will focus on the positive and stay happy. You can choose to do the same thing any time you encounter a similar situation.

Do You Need a Fix?

When I say "do you need a fix," I am not talking about drugs. I am talking about a fresh fix of strokes from people making you feel important just to get through every day. When we don't know our value in God, we look to other people to make us feel valuable; however, they don't always know what we need, and even if they did, they might not know how to give it to us.

Now that I see clearly, I realize that the majority of Dave's and my problems in the early years of our marriage were due to the difference in our personalities, or to my having expectations that he didn't realize I had. In marriage we seem to want our spouses to be mind readers and always know what we want, but they don't. How often do you get hurt because you assume someone has enough common sense to know what you want, but that person doesn't? If we fear rejection we may be reluctant to state our need clearly. We may drop a hint, but we don't want to clearly tell someone what we need just in case that person rejects us.

Many Tears

I shed many tears over the years because Dave was going to play golf and I "expected" him to stay home and pay attention to me, or to ask me what I wanted to do that day. I wouldn't ask him to stay home and do something with me, but instead I wanted him to "want" to, or to know that he should. I wanted him to sacrifice his desires for me so I would feel loved and valuable.

One day after crying most of the day and being completely miserable I finally thought, "This is stupid I know Dave loves me and that he would never hurt me intentionally, so why do I feel so utterly crushed?" The answer was that I was still reacting to the root of rejection. I still didn't know God's love deeply enough to make me know my value, so I needed a "fix" from Dave. Sadly, I needed one almost daily, and that pressured him.

I am asking you to be very honest with yourself and try to see clearly regarding any difficulty you may have in relationships. Are they connected to the way you feel about yourself? And if so, is it really fair to ask someone else to keep you fixed all the time? I believe we must take responsibility for our own happiness, because nobody else can keep us happy all the time, and they shouldn't have to.

You Hurt My Feelings!

How often have you said to someone, "You hurt my feelings," and had that person reply, "I wasn't trying to hurt your feelings"? It used to happen between Dave and me on a regular basis. I will relate two personal examples that I shared in my book *The Root of Rejection.*

Dave and I were playing golf together and he was having a really rough day. If you know anything about golf, you know that a person can be a really good golfer and still have days when he cannot seem to do anything right. Dave was having one of those days. As I have a mothering instinct, I felt really sorry for him, and while riding down the fairway in the golf cart, I patted him on the back and said, "You'll get a breakthrough and everything will be fine!" He responded, "Don't feel sorry for me; this is good for me! You just wait and see, when I come through this, I will play better than ever before!" When Dave wouldn't receive my comfort I was once again crushed. I literally felt as if I had collapsed on the inside. I thought, "You are so pigheaded! You never need anyone to comfort you. Why couldn't you have appreciated my comfort?" Still hurt and seething inside with anger, I was driving home in silence when the Lord whispered in my heart, "Joyce, you are trying to give Dave what you would need in this situation, and he doesn't need that, so he didn't receive it." I realized that I felt rejected because I expected him to need what I needed, and he didn't. His personality is different from mine and he didn't have a root of rejection in his life.

Another lesson for me occurred while Dave and I were at the post office. Dave had come out of the post office, and I started to tell him something that was important to me. I was into my story and noticed that Dave wasn't paying attention to me. He said, "Look at that man coming out of the post office! His shirt is ripped all the way down the back!"

I said, "Dave, I am trying to talk to you about something important." And he said, "Well, I just wanted you to look at the man's shirt." I felt he was more interested in the man's ripped shirt than he was in me, and once again I felt the crushing pain of what I viewed as rejection. The entire episode was a simple difference in our personalities and had nothing at all to do with Dave rejecting me. He is a "watcher," and I am a "doer." Dave loves to watch things and people, and he notices all the details. I wasn't interested in the man or his ripped shirt, I was only interested in reaching my goal, and that was telling Dave what I wanted to tell him.

When Rebecca was a little girl, she was a bit like Dennis the Menace, full of good intentions but always getting into trouble. It seemed that no matter what she did, something always ended up going wrong, and it was always her fault. It got to the point that whenever anything went wrong, Rebecca's mom and dad always just assumed that it was Rebecca's fault. Usually they were right, but sometimes they were mistaken.

On many occasions, Rebecca's mom would walk into the kitchen and see some water spilled on the floor, or she would see a snag in the upholstery of a chair. Whatever she found wrong, she just assumed that Rebecca was the culprit. As a result, there were many times over the years when Rebecca would get punished for something she actually hadn't done. I'm sure her parents didn't mean to harm her, but their undeserved punishments made a huge, negative impact on Rebecca.

When Rebecca was a grown married woman, sometimes her husband would say, "There's a spill on the floor," or, "There's some paint scraped off the car." Immediately Rebecca would tense up and snap, "I didn't do it!"

Finally one day her husband looked at her in wonder and said, "You must have had a rough childhood. Every time I ever mention anything that's wrong, you immediately think I'm blaming you."

That was the day Rebecca realized that when someone commented on a problem, that person wasn't necessarily accusing her of causing it. Rebecca was forty-three when she had that realization. What a sad thing that she had experienced countless episodes of feeling falsely accused, when the supposed "accuser" was actually just making an observation.

It is amazing how we view situations when we are looking through a lens colored by a root of rejection. It causes us a lot of pain that no one intends to give us. We get hurt and nobody is intending to hurt us. I believe that as we all learn to see more clearly we can avoid a lot of this type of pain and the tension it causes in relationships.

When you feel hurt, stop and think! Are people trying to hurt you, or are they just being who they are? Yes, maybe they could be more thoughtful or sensitive, but since none of us is perfect, we can choose to believe the best and move on.

Don't let the pain of past rejection rule your future. Face it, deal with it, pray about it and ask God to change you, study God's Word, and press forward! Even if you feel very convicted as you read these areas I am writing about, just remember that receiving conviction is a healthy step toward change. You don't need to feel condemned. God is not disappointed in you! He knew all about your weaknesses long before you did.

CHAPTER 8

Guilt and Shame

And, beloved, if our consciences (our hearts) do not accuse us [if they do not make us feel guilty and condemn us], we have confidence (complete assurance and boldness) before God.

1 John 3:21

Guilt can be healthy or unhealthy. If it is the feeling we get when we have done something wrong, then that is healthy. It reminds us that we need to ask for God's forgiveness, or perhaps a person's forgiveness. Unhealthy guilt is a false guilt. It is one that lingers even after we have asked for forgiveness. It can also be the result of an oversensitive conscience that causes feelings of guilt over things that are not wrong except in our own thoughts. This type of wrong and unhealthy guilt is what we will deal with in this chapter. I think I can safely say that I suffered more with feelings of guilt in my life than any other thing.

In *The Phantom Limb*, Dr. Paul Brand provides a vivid image of the impact of unhealthy guilt.

> *Amputees often experience some sensation of a phantom limb. Somewhere, locked in their brains, a memory lingers of the nonexistent hand or leg. Invisible toes curl, imaginary hands grasp things, a "leg" feels so sturdy a patient may try*

to stand on it. For a few, the experience includes pain. Doc-
tors watch helplessly, for the part of the body screaming for
attention does not exist. One such patient was my medical
school administrator, Mr. Barwick, who had a serious and
painful circulation problem in his leg but refused to allow the
recommended amputation. As the pain grew worse, Barwick
grew bitter. "I hate it!" he would mutter about the leg. At last
he relented and told the doctor, "I can't stand it anymore.
I'm through with that leg. Take it off." Surgery was sched-
uled immediately. Before the operation, however, Barwick
proceeded with a bizarre request: "I would like you to pre-
serve my leg in a pickling jar. I will install it on my mantel
shelf. Then as I sit in my armchair, I will taunt the leg, 'Hah!
You can't hurt me anymore!'" Ultimately, he got his wish. But
the despised leg had the last laugh. Barwick suffered phan-
tom limb pain of the worst degree. The wound healed, but he
could feel the torturous pressure of the swelling as the mus-
cles cramped, and he had no prospect of relief. He had hated
the leg with such intensity that the pain had unaccountably
lodged permanently in his brain.

To me, phantom leg pain provides wonderful insight into the
phenomenon of false guilt. Christians can be obsessed by the
memory of some sin committed years ago. It never leaves them,
crippling their ministry, their devotional life, and their relationships with others. They live in the fear that someone will discover
their past. They work overtime trying to prove to God they're
repentant. They erect barriers against the enveloping, loving
grace of God. Unless they experience the truth in 1 John 3:19–20
that God is "greater than our consciences," they become as pitiful
as poor Mr. Barwick, shaking his hand in fury at the pickled leg
on the mantel.

It is tormenting to live life with a burden of guilt. Jesus bore our sins and the guilt associated with them, and in reality, once we have received forgiveness for any sin we have committed, there is no longer any guilt. When sin goes, guilt goes with it. Jesus not only forgives sin, He removes it completely. He remembers it no more, and to Him, it is as if it never happened. When we feel guilt after we have confessed and repented of a sin, we should tell the feeling that it is a lie. Don't let your feelings be the ruling factor in your life. The Bible says that we are justified in Christ, and I heard one theologian say that means that we stand before God just as if we had never sinned. Even if our feelings can't believe it, we can choose to live beyond our feelings and we can honor God's Word above how we feel. If we make right choices according to the Word of God, our feelings will eventually come in line with our good choices.

I like what Jerry Bridges said about guilt and conscience, or feeling guilty:

"There are two 'courts' we must deal with: The court of God in Heaven and the court of conscience in our souls. When we first trust in Christ for salvation, God's court is forever satisfied. Never again will a charge of guilt be brought against us in Heaven. Our consciences, however, are continually pronouncing us guilty. That is the function of conscience. Therefore we must by faith bring the verdict of conscience into line with the verdict of Heaven. We do this by agreeing with our conscience about our guilt, but then reminding it that our guilt has already been borne by Christ."

Since all have sinned and are falling short of the honor and glory which God bestows and receives.

[All] are justified and made upright and in right standing with God, freely and gratuitously by His grace (His

unmerited favor and mercy), through the redemption which is
[provided] in Christ Jesus.

Romans 3:23–24

If you pass over what I said quickly, you may not get the full-ness of the power and freedom found in it. Let's go over it again, but this time slowly.

1. Once we have asked for and received forgiveness for any sin we have committed, there is no longer any guilt. If we feel guilt after that, it is false guilt.
2. When Jesus forgives sin it is completely removed and He remembers it no more. It is as if it had never happened.
3. We are justified through faith in Jesus and that means we stand before God just as if we had never sinned.
4. This promise is for all who are redeemed in Christ.
5. When your conscience makes you feel guilty, remind it that although you have sinned, you have also been for-given and made right with God.

I like the part of Romans 3:23 that says we are all "falling" short of God's glory. We did not just fall one time, but we are always falling, and the forgiveness that God offers in Christ is continual. It is not a one-time thing, but it is available any time we need it.

I have been offered once-in-a-lifetime deals, and I have found they are not always as good as they sound. They are usually intended to move us emotionally to make a quick decision so we don't miss this marvelous once-in-a-lifetime, never-to-be-repeated opportunity.

What God offers us in Christ is not like that at all. It is available for anyone, any time they need it! Jesus, the substitutionary atonement, paid our penalty. He became guilty so that we could become innocent. He was guilty of no sin, yet He took on Himself the guilt of us all (Isaiah 53:11).

Satan is called "the accuser of our brethren" in Revelation 12:10, and that is exactly what he is. He accuses us as if we are still guilty of things that we have been forgiven for.

Unwelcome Reminders

How long will you let Satan, the accuser of God's children, make a slave of you?

Steven Cole tells a story on Higherpraise.com that is humorous, but it makes an important point about becoming someone else's slave.

> A little boy was visiting his grandparents and was given his first slingshot. He practiced in the woods, but he could never hit a target. As he came back to Grandma's back yard, he spied her pet duck. On an impulse he took aim and let a rock fly. The stone hit, and the duck fell dead. The boy panicked. His sister Sally had seen it all, but she said nothing.
>
> After lunch that day, Grandma said, "Sally, let's wash the dishes." But Sally said, "Johnny told me he wanted to help in the kitchen today. Didn't you Johnny?" And she whispered to him, "Remember the duck!" So Johnny did the dishes.
>
> Later Grandpa asked if the children wanted to go fishing. Grandma said, "I'm sorry, but I need Sally to help make supper." Sally smiled and said, "That's all taken care of. Johnny wants to do it!" Again she whispered, "Remember the duck." Johnny stayed while Sally went fishing. After several days of Johnny doing both his chores and Sally's, finally he couldn't

stand it. He confessed to Grandma that he'd killed the duck. "I know, Johnny," she said, giving him a hug. "I was standing at the window and saw the whole thing. Because I love you, I forgave you. I wondered how long you would let Sally make a slave of you."

Satan is a liar, but one of his favorite weapons of torment is to merely remind us of past sins. He is vigilant in his efforts to make us cower under the weight of our own shame. Guilt and shame make us feel that God is angry, and we withdraw from His presence and live weak, pitiful lives.

We all sin and come short of the glory of God. No person is without sin, and we all feel guilt at times, but when we keep the guilt long after we have been forgiven, it turns to shame. We feel guilt over what we have done, but we feel ashamed of ourselves.

Satan has a good memory. He remembers every tiny thing that each of us has ever done wrong and brings unwelcome reminders. God has not only forgiven us, but has forgotten our sins and remembers them no more. We must stop remembering what God has forgotten. When Satan reminds us of a past sin, we should open our mouth and say, "I don't know what you are talking about. I don't remember doing that." Or, at the very least we should say, "Thanks for the reminder. It helps me recall how great God's mercy is toward me and how thankful I am for complete forgiveness."

I am using the term "complete forgiveness" frequently because I want to stress that God's forgiveness is not partial, or almost, but it is complete. When someone has sinned against us, we may forgive a little, but still hold some kind of grudge. This is, of course, not true forgiveness at all. The God kind of forgiveness is complete. Take a moment and think of the worst thing you can remember that you have ever done. Now, realize that you are *completely* forgiven. The goodness of God is greater than any bad thing we have ever done or could ever do. That should bring a sigh of relief and a sensation of joy sweeping through your soul.

God goes to great lengths in His Word to inform us that in Christ we are new creatures, old things have passed away and all things have become new (2 Corinthians 5:17). We are offered a brand-new way of living. We have newness of life. A new covenant with God sealed in the blood of Jesus. Jesus gave us one new commandment: that we should love one another as He loves us. Everything that God offers is new. Every old thing must be left behind. Your future has no room in it for your past mistakes. Actually, your future is so bright that you should need sunglasses to look at it.

We must leave behind old ways of thinking and old behavior patterns. We put off the old man and put on the new man. We no longer live under the old covenant of law, works, sin and death. We are instructed to let go of what lies behind in order to make way for the new. Jesus said that new wine could not be poured into old wineskins. The new life that God has for us has no room in it for the old. Just doing a Bible study on all the things that God has made new is very encouraging. Are you holding on to old things while at the same time trying to live a new life in Christ? If so, you will only feel frustrated and defeated. Every day can be a new beginning.

Satan tries desperately to keep us stuck in the past, feeling guilty for old things and reminding us of all our faults, weaknesses and shortcomings. Make a decision that you are going to start fresh each day, letting go of what lies behind and rejoicing in the day God has given you.

Earlier in the book we talked about God's character. It is easy for Satan to deceive us if we don't know God's character. Once again, let me say that He is not like people. Most of our guilt is caused by what we think about God's expectations and the way we think about sin and its remedy.

Sin is only a problem if we refuse to admit it and confess it. It is spiritually healthy and emotionally freeing to simply agree with God, take responsibility for our wrong actions, receive the free gift of forgiveness and ask Him to help us change.

> *If we [freely] admit that we have sinned and confess our sins, He is faithful and just [true to His own nature and promises] and will forgive our sins [dismiss our lawlessness] and [continuously] cleanse us from all unrighteousness [everything not in conformity to His will in purpose, thought, and action].*
>
> 1 John 1:9

If we will face what God already knows, that we are flawed and imperfect sinners who need Him every moment that we live, then sin is not a problem. If one of my grandchildren spills something on the floor, I quickly say, "Don't worry, it's not a problem. Grandma can clean it up. I have something that will make the floor clean again." I have noticed that sometimes when they spill something, they immediately look frightened, as if they are going to be in trouble. So I tell them not to worry as quickly as I can because I don't want them to feel bad because they made a mistake.

When we make mistakes, Jesus feels the same way. It is as if He is saying, "Don't worry, I have just the thing to clean up your mess, and it won't even leave a stain." When sin is removed and cleansed with the blood of Jesus, it should leave no guilty stain!

God doesn't expect us not to make mistakes. He already knows about every mistake we will ever make, and He has already decided to forgive us. Sin does have to be paid for, but we don't have to pay! What if you went to the electric company to pay your bill and they looked up your account and said, "Someone paid your bill in full yesterday." How foolish would it be if you kept standing there trying to pay the bill that had already been paid? That is exactly what we do sometimes concerning our sin. We ask God to forgive us, He does, and yet we keep trying to pay with feelings of guilt. We must learn to ask and receive. Asking is one step, but receiving completes the process. We are to ask and receive that our joy might be full (John 16:24).

If we don't know how to receive the free gift of God's merciful grace, then we will punish ourselves with guilt. We sacrifice our peace and joy, but our sacrifices are not acceptable to God because they are not enough. Only Jesus could pay the price that had to be paid. Only He could become the perfect, sinless sacrifice for our sins. Stop trying to pay a debt that you cannot pay.

Leaving the City of Regret

I have told this story before, but it needs to be repeated here because it is so good. It is an allegory about regrets that brings to life the importance of choosing your destinations carefully!

> I had not really planned on taking a trip this time of year, and yet I found myself packing rather hurriedly. This trip was going to be unpleasant and I knew in advance that no real good would come of it. I'm talking about my annual "Guilt Trip."

I got tickets to fly there on Wish I Had Airlines. It was an extremely short flight. I got my baggage, which I could not check. I chose to carry it myself all the way. It was weighted down with a thousand memories of what have been. No one greeted me as I entered the terminal to the Regret City International Airport. I say international because people from all over the world come to this dismal town.

As I checked into the Last Resort Hotel, I noticed that they would be hosting the year's most important event, the Annual Pity Party. I wasn't going to miss that great social occasion. Many of the town's leading citizens would be there.

First, there would be the Done family, Should Have Done, Would Have Done, and Could Have Done. Then came the I Had family. You probably know ol' Wish I Had and his clan. Of course, the Opportunities would be present, Missed and Lost. The biggest family would be the Yesterdays. There are far too many of them to count, but each one would have a very sad story to share.

Then Shattered Dreams would surely make an appearance. And It's Their Fault would regale us with stories (excuses) about how things had failed in his life, and each story would be loudly applauded by Don't Blame Me and I Couldn't Help It.

Well, to make a long story short, I went to this depressing party knowing that there would be no real benefit in doing so. And, as usual, I became very depressed. But as I thought about all of the stories of failures brought back from the past, it occurred to me that all of this trip and subsequent "pity party" trips could be canceled by me! I started to truly realize that I did not have to be there. I didn't have to be depressed. One thing kept going through my mind: I CAN'T CHANGE YESTERDAY, BUT I DO HAVE THE POWER TO MAKE

TODAY A WONDERFUL DAY. I can be happy, joyous, ful-filled, encouraged, as well as encouraging. Knowing this, I left the City of Regret immediately and left no forwarding address. Am I sorry for mistakes I've made in the past? YES! But there is no physical way to undo them.

So, if you're planning a trip back to the City of Regret, please cancel all your reservations now. Instead, take a trip to a place called Starting Again. I liked it so much that I have now taken up permanent residence there. My neighbors, the I Forgive Myselfs and the New Starts, are so very helpful. By the way, you don't have to carry around heavy baggage, because the load is lifted from your shoulders on arrival. God bless you in finding this great town. If you have difficulty finding it—it's in your own heart—please look me up. I live on I Can Do It Street.

Imagination

We all have an area of our thought life called "imagination." That's where we see mental images of how we believe things are. The images can be correct or incorrect. If you see yourself as a failure, when you're actually a forgiven child of God—then you have an imagination that needs to be renewed. The Bible teaches us to pull down mental strongholds and put down imaginations that don't agree with God's Word. It is our job, with the Holy Spirit's help, to bring every thought into captivity to the obedi-ence of Christ (2 Corinthians 10:4–5). In simple terms, we must learn to think and imagine as God does if we want to see His good plan for us come to pass. You can think or imagine things on purpose. You don't have to merely passively wait to see what falls into your mind and then meditate on it over and over until it becomes part of you. God puts things in our mind, but Satan also puts things into our mind, and it is vital that we know the source of our thoughts and imaginings.

Often when I am preparing to teach God's Word, I imagine or see myself in front of the people, and I preach the sermon in my mind before I arrive at the church or conference center. I believe this helps me prepare.

I am on my way home right now and haven't seen Dave for a few days, so I am looking forward to seeing him. We are going from the airport to lunch, and several times I have seen a picture in my mind of the restaurant we are going to and of ordering the meal we always get when we go there. I can see us enjoying the time and catching up on what has happened to both of us while we have been apart. My daughter's birthday is today, and I have imagined how she will like her birthday gift when I give it to her.

Our imaginations and mind prepare us for action. They can prepare us for success or failure, joy or misery, and the choice is up to us. If you think about the past mistakes and all the things you have done wrong, it will only weaken you. It handicaps you as you try to enter the future God has for you. No matter what you have done in the past, learn to see yourself as a new creature in Christ. See what you want to happen, not just more of what you have always had.

Meditating on the past stirs up false guilt and will eventually become a stronghold in your mind. A stronghold is an area where the enemy has dug in and buried himself. It is much more difficult to tear down a stronghold than it is to form the habit of saying "no" to wrong thoughts each time they present themselves.

We need to stop thinking about our past failures if we want to defeat and overcome guilt and shame. We must stop focusing on the sin that has been forgiven and dealt with, and begin to praise God, thanking Him for the solution to the problem. Think about how wonderful it is to be completely forgiven. Here are a few

Scriptures to meditate on that will help you defeat Satan when he comes to you with false guilt.

> *Bless (affectionately, gratefully praise) the Lord, O my soul, and forget not [one of] all His benefits—*
>
> *Who forgives [every one of] all your iniquities, Who heals [each one of] all your diseases,*
>
> *Who redeems your life from the pit and corruption, Who beautifies, dignifies, and crowns you with loving-kindness and tender mercy.*
>
> Psalm 103:2–4

> *As far as the east is from the west, so far has He removed our transgressions from us.*
>
> Psalm 103:12

> *Come now, and let us reason together, says the Lord. Though your sins are like scarlet, they shall be as white as snow; though they are red like crimson, they shall be like wool.*
>
> Isaiah 1:18

> *There is therefore now no condemnation to them which are in Christ Jesus.*
>
> Romans 8:1 (KJV)

> *If we confess our sins, he is faithful and just to forgive us our sins, and to cleanse us from all unrighteousness.*
>
> 1 John 1:9 (KJV)

Meditating on Scripture is the best way to defend yourself against mental attacks from the devil.

Shame

It is one thing to be ashamed of something you have done wrong, but it is another thing entirely to become ashamed of yourself. Shame is actually much deeper and more damaging than guilt. I was not able to heal from the abuse in my childhood until I realized that I had toxic shame filling my soul. I was ashamed of who I was and it poisoned everything in my life.

I am sure that at the beginning of my father's sexual abuse toward me I was ashamed of what he was doing, and I clearly remember feeling guilty, even though I was too small to understand why I felt that way. At some point, as the abuse continued, I took the shame inside myself, and I became ashamed of me because he was abusing me. I thought that something was dreadfully wrong with me for my father to want to do the things that he was doing to me. He told me that what he was doing was good and that he did it because he loved me so much. Yet, he always warned me over and over not to tell anyone, so it made no sense to me. If what he was doing was good, as he told me it was, then why couldn't I tell anyone? And if it was so good, then why wasn't everyone doing it? I was pretty sure they weren't. As I said, I felt confused about all of it and had no answers, but I was deeply ashamed of myself and felt certain that something was desperately wrong with me! The soundtrack "What is wrong with me? What is wrong with me? What is wrong with me?" played over and over in my head until I was in my mid forties. Then I found out about the devastating effects of shame and with God's help was set free from it.

Over the many years of abuse, I had developed a shame-based nature, and as long as that is the case, people can never fully get over feeling guilty. They will not only feel guilt over real offenses, but they frequently feel guilty about imagined offenses. Anything that was even remotely enjoyable made me feel guilty and as if I had no right to enjoy myself. The shame distorted everything in my life. It was as if I was wearing glasses with mud on the lenses, and everything looked dirty to me because I felt dirty inside.

If this is a problem for you, I have wonderful news! Jesus has taken away the reproach of sin (the guilt and shame). He bore your shame and guilt. He has declared you *not guilty* and made you a brand-new creation in Christ (2 Corinthians 5:17). When you feel condemned, it is not Jesus condemning you; it is the devil, and you must resist him. When you are having a guilt-and-shame attack, you must remember who you are in Christ. I recommend saying out loud, "God loves me unconditionally, and He has forgiven all of my sins."

We are nothing in and of ourselves, but in Christ we are forgiven, made new, justified, sanctified, cleansed, and we stand before God right with Him. God is not angry with you; He is not disappointed or displeased. He loves you! I am sure you did a good job at receiving guilt and condemnation; now do a better job at receiving righteousness from God through Christ.

CHAPTER 9

Religion

Some people have just enough religion to make themselves miserable.

Harry Emerson Fosdick

Religion gives us rules to follow, and it promises that if we follow those rules, God will be pleased with us. The problem is that we cannot follow them all, and if we are guilty of breaking one, God views us as guilty of breaking all (James 2:10). If we choose to live by religious legalism and a rule-keeping system, then weakness is simply not an option, so we struggle to be strong in every area, yet we always fail. If we fail to keep all the rules, then we feel we have sinned, and we experience all the misery and guilt of sin. We also have a feeling of being separated from God. God never leaves us, but our guilt places a wedge between us and Him. When we have a false view of what God expects from us, it opens the door for a lifetime of seeking something we can never attain and it produces tremendous frustration and disappointment.

On the other hand, Jesus offers us the exact opposite of religion. He offers us a new heart, a new nature and an intimate relationship with God through Him. This is all ours through placing our faith in Him. If we believe what God's Word teaches us about what Jesus did for us, we receive these promises and they set us free from the tyranny of trying to earn God's love and acceptance through our own performance.

> Therefore if any person is [ingrafted] in Christ (the Messiah) he is a new creation (a new creature altogether); the old [previous moral and spiritual condition] has passed away. Behold, the fresh and new has come!
>
> 2 Corinthians 5:17

Jesus shows us how to live by example, gives us a desire to do it, and through the power of the Holy Spirit He enables, strengthens and helps us. When we realize what God has done for us through Jesus and we learn to receive His amazing unconditional love, we love Him in return and we want to please Him by being like Him and doing what we believe He would do in every situation. Wanting to do something and making an effort because of desire is entirely different from feeling the pressure of having to do something out of obligation and being afraid if we don't.

Religion says, "You have to do these things," but it gives you no power to do them. Jesus says, "I will give you a new desire; I will cause you to want to do the right things and I will even enable you to do them." Now I ask you, which of these two plans sounds the best to you? The law says, "These are the rules to follow." But it gives us no help in doing the right thing. Jesus gives us a desire to do right and then sends us a Helper, the Holy Spirit, Who remains with us all of our life to strengthen, enable, convict, convince, teach us, and pray through us (John 14:26). One system puts us at rest, while the other is a heavy burden. Religion produces bondage, but Jesus gives us grace, righteousness, peace and joy.

There was once a couple who didn't really love each other. The husband was very demanding, so much so that he prepared a list of rules and regulations for his wife to follow. He insisted that she read them over every day and obey them to the letter. His "dos and don'ts" included what time she had to get up in the morning, when his breakfast should be served, and how the housework should be done. After several years, the husband died. As time passed, the woman fell in love with another man, one who dearly loved her. Soon they were married. This husband did everything he could to make his new wife happy, continually showering her with loving words and tokens of his appreciation. One day as she was cleaning house, she found tucked away in a drawer the list of commands her first husband had drawn up for her. As she looked it over, it dawned on her that even though her present husband hadn't given her any kind of list, she was doing everything her first husband's list required anyway. She realized she was so devoted to her present husband that her deepest desire was to please him out of love, not obligation.

Jesus did not die for us so we could have a religion of rules and regulations, but in order that through Him we might enjoy an intimate relationship with the Father, Son and Holy Spirit. We all need to ask ourselves if we have religion or relationship. For many years I had religion. I went to church, I learned the rules (law), and tried very hard to keep them. Of course I broke them all the time and I was frustrated and disappointed. I wanted to keep them so I could feel good about myself and believe that God was not mad at me and that He accepted me, but since I failed most of the time, I usually felt bad about myself and lived with the vague feeling that God was not pleased with me. Does that sound familiar?

On rare occasions when I did have a few good days, I felt proud of myself and gave myself the credit for my supposed goodness. We all have some things we are good at; however, if we are religious, we'll likely judge others who are not as good at them as we are. But if we know that any good we do is Christ working in and through us, then we give Him the credit. Being fully aware of our own inability to do everything right enables us to be merciful toward other people when they make mistakes.

The entire system of religion has been devastating to the cause of Christ and has actually driven many people away from God rather than drawing them to Him.

Two Kinds of Religion

The nineteenth-century Danish theologian Søren Kierkegaard identified two kinds of religion—religion A and religion B. The first is "faith" in name only (2 Timothy 3:5). It's the practice of attending church without genuine faith in the living Lord. Religion B, on the other hand, is a life-transforming, destiny-changing experience. It's a definite commitment to the crucified and risen Savior, which establishes an ongoing personal relationship between a forgiven sinner and a gracious God.

Kierkegaard goes on to say that C. S. Lewis had great difficulty in becoming a Christian because religion A had blinded him to religion B. The apostle Paul said that he had to die to the law in order to live to and for Christ (Galatians 2:19). C. S. Lewis's childhood had given him what he referred to as a spiritual illness through compulsory church during his school days and the dryness of religion offered by a semipolitical church.

Many young people have a bad experience with religion early in life, and it often causes them to reject anything that hints of religion or church. They may have had religious parents who were very legalistic in their expectations of their children, and the damage done to such children can be devastating. If they never learn the difference between religion and an intimate relationship with God through Christ, they will suffer the agony of separation from God throughout their lifetime.

My own father had a similar experience. His father was very religious, but very mean. He was harsh, rigid and legalistic, but he went to church twice a week. This experience was very damaging to my father's view of God and religion. He always had the opinion that churchgoing people were hypocritical, because that had been his experience early in life. He grew up bitter and never got over it, so he became mean and abusive like his own father was.

We should all ask ourselves if we have religion A or religion B, and make sure we have the right one. If we don't, it will harm not only us, but the people we influence as well.

Not only are there two kinds of religion, there are also two kinds of righteousness. The first, righteousness A, is a righteousness that we try to earn through our good works. The second, righteousness B, is the righteousness of God that is given as a free gift to those who sincerely believe in Jesus. Righteousness A causes struggle and frustration and fruitlessness, but righteousness B allows us to rest in God and appreciate His love and mercy.

Jesus invites people who are striving for works-based righteousness to give it up and receive faith-based righteousness.

> Come to Me, all you who labor and are heavy-laden and overburdened, and I will cause you to rest. [I will ease and relieve and refresh your souls.]

Take My yoke upon you and learn of Me, for I am gentle (meek) and humble (lowly) in heart, and you will find rest (relief and ease and refreshment and recreation and blessed quiet) for your souls.

For My yoke is wholesome (useful, good—not harsh, hard, sharp, or pressing, but comfortable, gracious, and pleasant), and My burden is light and easy to be borne.

Matthew 11:28–30

My own struggle to keep the rules and earn righteousness A was intense and caused many years of agony. My entire view of God was wrong. I saw Him as a demanding God who gave us rules to follow and was angry when we didn't. I was trying to get to God through my good behavior and always sensed that I was falling short of my goal. Through studying God's Word and with the help of the Holy Spirit as my teacher, I finally learned about righteousness B, and that is the righteousness received through faith in Christ.

For no person will be justified (made righteous, acquitted, and judged acceptable) in His sight by observing the works prescribed by the Law. For [the real function of] the Law is to make men recognize and be conscious of sin [not mere perception, but an acquaintance with sin which works toward repentance, faith, and holy character].

But now the righteousness of God has been revealed independently and altogether apart from the Law, although actually it is attested by the Law and the Prophets,

Namely, the righteousness of God which comes by believing with personal trust and confident reliance on Jesus Christ (the Messiah). [And it is meant] for all who believe. For there is no distinction.

Romans 3:20–22

God doesn't give us a list of rules to follow and then stand on the sidelines watching us fail, but He gives us a new heart and then helps us do all that He has given us a desire to do. We must learn to depend entirely on Jesus to give us right standing with God and to help us do what is right in His sight. We should form the habit of leaning on God in all things. The cardinal guideline for the Christian who wants to be what God wants him to be is, "Apart from Me you can do nothing" (John 15:5). The apostle John compares our relationship with Christ to the relationship between the vine and the branch. All the life and growth potential of the branch is in the vine, and may only be received by the branch if it remains in the vine. The branch is entirely dependent on the vine for everything it needs to grow and bear fruit. This is a beautiful analogy of how our life with Christ should be.

Keeping the Law Never Produces Good Fruit

The apostle Paul was a rule-keeping religious Pharisee, and yet Scripture teaches us that he was persecuting Christians. Isn't it interesting that religiously legalistic people will persecute true Christians? Paul finally saw the light and eventually chose to be found and known as in Christ, not having any self-achieved supposed righteousness that was based on the law's demands, but possessing that genuine righteousness which comes through faith in Christ (Philippians 3:9).

Many years ago, I was hosting a seminar in my city and my daughter asked the manager of the mobile home park she lived in at the time if she could put flyers on the mailboxes. She received permission, and the only complaint she got was from a woman who was known to be very religious. Although the woman didn't know me at all, she formed a negative opinion simply because I wasn't exactly like her. I am sure she followed all the rules of her particular religious sect and yet she did not display the fruit of the Holy Spirit toward me.

I can truthfully say that some of the deepest hurts I have experienced in my life have come from religious rule-keeping people, who did not walk in love. If we think we have no faults, then we find fault with almost everyone else. But if we know we need forgiveness, then we will be able to give it away. If we know we need mercy and long-suffering patience from God, we will be able to give it to others. It is impossible to give away what we have not first received from God.

A religious attitude is one of the worst that anyone can have. It always comes across to others as superior and critical. Jesus said that religious people can easily tell others what to do, but they don't always do it themselves. They also place heavy burdens on others by demanding that they perform perfectly, but then they won't even lift a finger to help. When they do good works, they do them in order to be seen, so even their motives for doing them are self-serving (Matthew 23:1–5).

We should pray that God will reveal the beauty of intimacy with Him and true righteousness to us. Don't ever be satisfied with a phony copy of the real thing that Jesus died to give you.

Extra Biblical Rules

God gave Moses ten commands to give to the people, but I have heard that by the time Jesus came, those ten had expanded into about twenty-two hundred. The thing we must realize about a legalistic religious system is that it is never satisfied. No amount of doing right is ever enough, so additional rules are constantly added. Matthew said that John neither ate nor drank with others, and the religious Pharisees said that he had a demon. Jesus came eating and drinking and they said He was a glutton (Matthew 11:18–19).

Satan has used their differing opinions of what those rules should be to divide the people of God. One young man told this story: "I am in earnest about forsaking 'the world' and following Christ. But I am puzzled about worldly things. What is it that I must forsake?" The answer came back, "Colored clothes for one thing. Get rid of everything in your wardrobe that is not white. Stop sleeping on a soft pillow. Sell your musical instruments and don't eat any more white bread. You cannot, if you are sincere about obeying Christ, take warm baths or shave your beard. To shave is to lie against Him who created us, to attempt to improve on His work."

Of course this sounds absurd, but it was the answer given by some of the most celebrated Christian schools of the second century! Elizabeth Elliot said, "Is it possible that the rules that have been adopted by many twentieth-century Christians will sound as absurd to earnest followers of Christ a few years from now?"

The list of extra biblical scruples has constantly shifted over the last eighteen hundred years. We desperately need to follow God's Word instead of the doctrines of man, unless those doctrines are in agreement with God's Word. Each person should know the Word of God for himself and never be totally dependent on what other people tell him. We must know God personally and not be satisfied with secondhand faith that we receive through someone else.

In Paul's letter to the Galatians, he charged them to remain free and not to be ensnared into legalism. He begged them to remain as he was, free of the bondage of ritualism and ordinances. He wanted them to be led by the Holy Spirit of God, and not by legalistic rule-keeping ordinances. He warned them to watch out for the evil persuasion of legalism that constantly looked for an opening in their lives. Paul said that even a little leaven of legalism could pervert the whole concept of faith and mislead the church. I urge you to study the book of Galatians for a healthy understanding of the difference between law and grace.

Jesus said that He was giving us one new commandment and that was to love one another just as He has loved us, and by that all men would know that we are His disciples (John 13:34–35). As I mentioned, I have heard that the Ten Commandments had developed into twenty-two hundred rules, but Jesus got it down to one thing: Focus on love! If we love wholeheartedly, we will fulfill the will of God and we will enjoy doing it.

"In contrast to the one command of Christ to love, the Pharisees had developed a system of 613 laws composed of 365 negative commands and 248 positive laws. By the time Christ came, that system had produced a heartless, cold and arrogant brand of righteousness. As such, it contained at least ten tragic flaws.

1. New laws continually need to be invented for new situations.
2. Accountability to God is replaced by accountability to men.
3. It reduces a person's ability to personally discern.
4. It creates a judgmental spirit.
5. The Pharisees confused personal preferences with divine law.
6. It produces inconsistencies.
7. It created a false standard of righteousness.
8. It became a burden to the Jews.
9. It was strictly external
10. It was rejected by Christ.

from *Fan The Flame*, J. Stowell

The story was told some years ago of a pastor who found the roads blocked one Sunday morning due to the river being frozen solid. He was forced to skate over the river to get to church. When he arrived at church the elders were horrified that their preacher had skated on the Lord's Day. After the service they held a meeting at which the pastor explained that it was either skate to church or not go at all. Finally one elder asked, "Did you enjoy it?" When the preacher answered, "No," the board decided it was all right!

Isn't that amazing? As long as the preacher had no fun on the Lord's Day, he could remain as pastor of the church. The thief of religion comes to steal and kill all of our joy, but Jesus came so that we could have and enjoy life abundantly (John 10:10). Religious rule-keeping people are almost always sour-faced and against all fun and enjoyment.

A man who works at our ministry as staff pastor shared with me that all of his life he had been a very jovial guy until he became religious. He said that he gradually became more and more legalistic until he had no fun at all and was no fun to be with. His wife actually asked him what happened to the fun guy she had married. Fortunately, he saw the truth and was freed from the bondage of legalism and has returned to his godly, yet fun-loving self.

Nothing can choke the heart and soul out of walking with God like legalism. God does want us to be disciplined people, but healthy discipline is a far cry from rigid legalism. Consider the story of Hans the tailor.

Because of his reputation, an influential entrepreneur visiting the city ordered a tailor-made suit. But when he came to pick up his suit, the customer found that one sleeve twisted that way and the other this way; one shoulder bulged out

and the other caved in. He pulled and managed to make his
body fit. As he returned home on the bus, another passen-
ger noticed his odd appearance and asked if Hans the tailor
had made the suit. Receiving an affirmative reply, the man
remarked, "Amazing! I knew that Hans was a good tailor,
but I had no idea he could make a suit fit so perfectly some-
one as deformed as you."

Often that is just what we do in the church. We get some idea of what the Christian faith should look like: then we push and shove people into the most grotesque configurations until they fit wonderfully! That is death. It is a wooden legalism which destroys the soul.

We must remember that God is not angry if we don't follow all the rules, because He isn't the One Who gave all the man-made rules to begin with. He gives new life and new desires. He enables us to follow Him from a new heart that is filled with a passion to please Him, not a fear of displeasing Him.

CHAPTER 10

Sad, Mad, or Glad?

Serve the Lord with gladness! Come before His presence with singing!

Psalm 100:2

There was once a young boy who went to spend the week with his grandfather on the farm. While walking around he noticed the chickens, they were scratching and playing around. The little lad said, "They ain't got it." Next he saw a colt in the field playing and kicking up its heels, to which he replied, "He ain't got it." After examining all the animals on his grandfather's farm and seeing that none of them had "it," this boy finally found the old donkey in the barn. When he saw the donkey's long, frowning face and the way that the donkey just sadly stood there he screamed for his grandfather to come quick. "I found it! I found it!" the boy kept yelling. When his grandfather asked what he had found he said, "Pawpaw, I found an animal that has the same kind of religion that you have."

Author unknown

Our relationship with God and the reality of what it means to be a forgiven and adored child of God should give us unimaginable joy, so why are so many people who claim to be Christians so sad? I believe it is because they do not understand the reality of being a new creation in Christ and the inheritance that is ours through our faith in Him. Until we understand the amazing things that God has done for us, we will always work to earn and deserve what God has already given by His grace as a free gift.

We will always be frustrated and disappointed because even our best effort at living a good life won't give us right standing with God. We will feel burned-out, weighed down and overburdened, and the result will be a total loss of true joy. We will end up mad and sad instead of being glad, as God desires us to be. The psalmist David spoke often of being glad; that was due to his accurate view of God and his intimate relationship with Him. In Psalm 16:11 David said, "In Your presence is fullness of joy." Obviously he wasn't afraid that God was mad at him or he would not have had joy in His presence.

> *You have turned my mourning into dancing for me; You have*
> *put off my sackcloth and girded me with gladness.*
>
> Psalm 30:11

This Scripture describes what our relationship with God should do for us. Are you glad? Do you have joy most of the time? On a scale of one to ten, what is your level of joy? After being a Christian and a minister for many years, I had to answer these questions for myself, and I realized that I was mad and sad more than I was glad. I also knew that had to change. I was a dedicated hard worker and very responsible, but I was not fully enjoying much of what I did. I wanted to do it, so why wasn't I enjoying it? It took me a few years to unpack all of my baggage and get to the root of my problem. Baggage is old assumptions and behaviors that we inevitably bring into new relationships. I brought baggage from my past into my relationship with Dave, and it took a long time for me to completely unpack it, and even now I sometimes find something neatly packed away that I had forgotten about and I have to deal with it. We bring our baggage into friendships, marriage and our relationship with God. We carry things from our past, such as pain, fears, insecurities, doubts, misunderstandings, defensiveness and expectations. We pack them up and carry them with us all the time, and they become heavy baggage indeed. We need to unpack our baggage. As we start confronting issues, we will leave sadness and anger behind and experience new levels of joy.

The single most important goal of this book is to unburden you of the baggage you have carried into your relationship with the Lord—hurt, bad teachings, flawed views of a father, a works-based faith, wrong fear of God and other things that are all heavy items of baggage that steal our joy.

Psalm 100 tells us to serve the Lord with gladness, and I think that is the least we can do after all He has done for us. Just imagine how you would feel if you did everything you possibly could to give your children a great life and they still refused to be glad and enjoy it. God has given us everything we need to enjoy Him, to enjoy ourselves and the life He has given us, and it is time we stop being mad or sad and get glad!

Why do so many people find that they lose their love of happiness when they begin to embrace the duty of religion? First of all, we should not see our relationship with God as a duty, but rather as a privilege. It is not something we have to be a part of, but something we are blessed and privileged to be a part of. It is also possible that we don't love and value happiness as we should.

As I searched for the roots of my lack of joy, one of the things I discovered was that I did not truly understand the great value and importance of joy. Joy is to our lives like gasoline is to an engine. Without gasoline, the engine will not run; without joy, I don't believe the human being runs well either. Joy gives us actual phys-ical energy—it provides the zeal and enthusiasm we need in our lives! According to the prophet Nehemiah, "The joy of the Lord is our Strength" (Nehemiah 8:10).

> Joy is to our lives like gasoline is to an engine. Without gasoline, the engine will not run; without joy, I don't believe the human being runs well either.

Without joy, everything is "down" (negative, dreary, flat and tasteless). Our thoughts are negative, our atti-tude is negative, our emotions are down (depressed) and even our head, shoulders and arms hang down, limp. Jesus did not die to give us a "down" life, but He is our glory and the lifter of our heads!

The more joy I have, the less tired I feel. Joy releases creativ-ity in me and it even seems to make me friendlier. I think a lack of joy is more of a problem than we realize. Statistics say that as many as 340 million people suffer from depression, and I read that in the United States alone someone tries to commit suicide every fourteen and one-half minutes. If we add to those numbers all the people who are sad and mad, that is a lot of unhappiness. You might be thinking, "Well Joyce, I wish I felt happier, and I am sure all those people wish they felt happier." We cannot pas-sively sit around and wish we felt joyful; we must take action and find out why we are unhappy. God has given us joy, so if we don't feel it, then we must have diluted it in some way to the point that it is no longer potent enough to flavor our lives.

If I have a glass of lemonade and start pouring glasses of water into it, I will dilute it to the point where it no longer tastes like lemonade at all. That is what I had done to my joy—and possibly what many people have done to theirs.

Joy Is a Gift from God

When we receive Jesus into our lives as our Savior, we receive all that He is into our spirit. We receive the Holy Spirit and all the fruit of the Spirit, including the fruit of joy.

> But the fruit of the [Holy] Spirit [the work which His presence within accomplishes] is love, joy (gladness), peace, patience (an even temper, forbearance), kindness, goodness (benevolence), faithfulness, gentleness (meekness, humility), self-control (self-restraint, continence).
>
> Galatians 5:22–23

This Scripture verifies that we have been given joy (gladness), as well as all the other fruit of the Holy Spirit. The first step in making use of anything is to believe that you have it. One could have a million dollars, but if one does not know one has it, one could live the life of a pauper. We have heard of cases like that and are all amazed by them. I can tell you there are more cases of spiritual paupers than of financial ones. Sad Christians are people who simply don't know what they have in Christ. They don't know what He has done for them. They have either never been informed or they have heard the truth but refuse to believe it could be true for them, because they think God is mad at them or that they don't deserve His blessings. Some people even believe that they don't deserve to be happy—so they never are.

It is my belief that only people who have a relationship with God can experience real joy. Other people may have various versions of happiness from time to time, but it comes and goes based on their circumstances. However, joy is a calm delight that we can have all the time regardless of our circumstances.

That is a gift from God and quite impossible to have any other way.

We have joy in us! First we need to believe we have it, and if we are not experiencing it, then we must ask ourselves what is diluting it.

Things That Dilute Joy

A wrong view of God will definitely dilute our joy. I just spoke with a woman and mentioned to her the title of this book. Her husband died suddenly about four years ago, and it has been very difficult for her to get beyond her grief. She was single until she was in her forties, and when she did get married, it was a wonderful relationship. But after ten years, her husband died in the hospital from an infection after a very simple surgery that should have been no problem at all. It was shocking, totally unexpected and devastating to her. When she heard the title of my book she said, "I have often wondered if God is angry at me because I have had such a hard time getting over my husband's death." This reaffirmed to me how important this message is. There may be even more people than I had imagined who suffer from this wrong view of God, thinking He is easily angered and disappointed with us most of the time unless we can react perfectly to every situation in life.

God is not angry with this woman, but He understands her pain. God is our Comforter, not our tormenter! Until we fully understand the character of God and have a proper view of Him, the fear of His not being pleased with us seems to be a poison that will permeate our thinking and compromise our lives. Just as the little boy understood the crippled puppy in the story I told earlier, God understands all of our pain, and He is the God of all Comfort Who comforts us in every affliction (2 Corinthians 1:3–4).

The devil will use just about anything to make us believe that God is mad at us, and to get us angry with ourselves. Here is another story that illustrates what I mean.

Francie has suffered from debilitating clinical depression that has lasted for months at a time during the course of her life. Doctors have established that this is depression due to inadequate synapses, or chemicals, in certain areas of her brain. While she has been able to earn a living and lead a relatively normal life, she has suffered terribly during many paralyzing episodes.

She tells of a time when she was a publicist for a famous actress. Francie's job was to book publicity tours for her boss to promote her career. At this particular time, a thirty-city tour was coming up, and Francie needed to call scores of television and radio shows, magazines and newspapers to arrange for them to cover the tour.

It happened that during that time, she was going through a major depression, She was barely even able to get herself dressed and to her office every day, much less set up a month-long publicity tour.

As she looked at thirty pages of empty itinerary just waiting to be filled, she tried to summon the wherewithal to start making phone calls, but she simply couldn't face the task. She started to berate herself. "You are so lazy," she thought to herself. "You're a poor excuse for a human being. You should be ashamed." On and on, she told herself what a miserable failure she was.

Francie, a committed Christian, gets a look of wonder on her face as she continues telling her story. Even now, years after the incident, she is obviously moved by what happened next.

"Out of nowhere, I began to 'hear' a question, not literally, but in my thinking. 'If you had a friend who suffered like you do and she was in your situation, how would you respond to her?'" Francie decided that she would feel sad for her friend who was in the middle of a crisis. "What if the person wasn't your friend but just an acquaintance?" she heard next. Francie knew that she would still feel sorry for that person. Then she heard a third question. "If that person was someone who had treated you terribly, who was mean and horrible to you, how would you feel?"

Even then, Francie knew, she would have a glimmer of compassion.

Francie will never forget what came to mind next: "So, if you just treated yourself as well as you would treat your worst enemy, you'd be better off than you are now."

Francie believes that the Holy Spirit was speaking to her that day, pointing out that we are so often our own worst judge. Jesus said to love our enemies. If we should love our enemies, then it stands to reason we should love ourselves, too.

It is only through Christ that we can do anything. Once we know that, we can accept that not only is God not mad at us, but we don't have to—nor should we—be mad at ourselves when we fall short. Francie's experience changed her view of God and how He deals with His children.

Bill Bright said, "Everything about our lives—our attitudes, motives, desires, actions, and even our words—is influenced by our view of God." A. W. Tozer said, "What comes into our minds when we think about God is the most important thing about us." Do you feel comfortable and relaxed when you think about God, or do you feel tense and even fearful? Because our view of God affects all of our choices, it can be compared to the foundation of a building. If the foundation is wrong, sooner or later, the building will collapse.

A mistaken view of God isn't a new problem. In the Old Testament, God's chosen people yielded to incorrect views of Him.

After they had been slaves in Egypt for many years, God led them out with a mighty hand and many amazing miracles. He parted the Red Sea and they crossed over on dry ground; He brought water out of a rock for them to drink, and He sent heavenly bread called manna from heaven each day for them to eat, and yet they still failed to see God as good and loving. "They grumbled against Moses and said, 'Why, now, have you brought us up from Egypt, to kill us and our children and our livestock with thirst?'" (Exodus 17:3 NASB). After all they had watched God do for them out of His goodness, they still viewed Him as angry and unkind. Wow! It is hard to believe how they, or, for that matter, we, could do that. But unless we know the true character of God and realize that He is only good all the time, we, too, find ourselves grumbling and complaining. It is absolutely essential to always remember that even when we don't get what we want or our circumstances seem to be difficult, God's intention is still good. He will work something good in us through the difficulty we're facing if we will continue to view Him correctly and put our trust in Him.

Some people may even erroneously believe that when they have problems in life it is because God is angry with them for some past sin. I have heard people say things like, "I had a miscarriage and I wonder if it is God punishing me for the way I lived in the past." Or, "I just found out I have cancer and I wonder if it is God punishing me for having an abortion when I was a teenager." Statements like this prove that these people have an incorrect view of God. He doesn't punish us for past sins by bringing bad things into our lives. Our troubles are not a sign that God is angry with us! We are in the world and Jesus said that in the world we would have tribulation. He also told us to cheer up because He had overcome the world (John 16:33).

More than twenty years ago, I had breast cancer that required surgery. The word "cancer" frightens all of us, but I recall that the first thing God spoke to my heart was to continue believing and saying, "God is good. He loves me, and this will work out for my good in the end." Staying positive and continuing to believe in the goodness of God during times of trial and tribulation will prevent the dilution of your joy.

Worry and anxiety will dilute our joy. God gives us the choice of casting all of our care on Him and believing that He will take care of us, or we can worry, which does no good at all, is a total waste of time and shows that we don't trust God. Worry and joy don't mix together well. After teaching God's Word for close to thirty-five years, I believe that teaching people not to worry is vital. But I don't think that any of us stop worrying until we have enough experience with God's faithfulness to realize that He is indeed better at problem-solving than we are.

Each difficulty in life that I have gone through has helped me go through the next one better. God is faithful, and relying on that releases joy in our lives. As I often say, "Worrying is like rocking back and forth in a rocking chair all day long; it keeps us busy, but gets us nowhere." The more we realize the infinite love of God for His people, the more we are able to stop worrying and trust Him in every kind of situation. Even when Jesus was painfully dying on the cross, He trusted Himself and everything to God because He knew that it was impossible for God to fail Him.

Reasoning is another thing that will dilute the joy of God in our lives. We all want answers, but many times God withholds understanding because He wants us to trust Him without it. We must learn to be joyful, knowing the One who *does* know all of the answers, rather than striving to know the answers ourselves. I recently read that "we live life forward, but unfortunately we can only understand it backward." How true that is. We can all look back on things that we let steal our peace and joy when they were happening and we say, "Now I understand what God was doing in that situation."

Giving up reasoning was very difficult for me because I wanted to be in charge and have no surprises in life. So I spent a great deal of time trying to figure things out. "Why, God, why?" was my most frequent prayer. Maybe you can relate to that. But once I did give up reasoning and let God take charge, my joy increased greatly.

Another thing that dilutes joy is being complicated. I believe we all need to simplify our approach to life. I doubt that life is going to get any simpler, but we can change the way we live it. For example, we don't have to keep up with everyone else. Your friend may be deep in debt in order to have a large home and an expensive car, but if an apartment and a smaller car fit your budget better, then you don't have to be in a competition. God is not requiring us to be anyone other than ourselves. We don't have to look like anyone else, or do as those others do. Learning to be your own amazing unique self is vital to have joy, and I will discuss it in detail in the next chapter.

Learning to forgive quickly and completely is one of the most important keys to maintaining joy in our lives. Because God has forgiven us, He expects us to forgive others for their injustices against us. I believe there are more people in the world who are angry with someone than there are those who aren't. It is a global dilemma. Satan gains more ground in people's lives through unforgiveness than any other thing. Just as we need to receive forgiveness from God and wholly believe that He is not angry with us, we also need to forgive others and not be angry with them. Anger will quickly and immediately dilute your joy. It is impossible to be angry and joyful at the same time.

Some people bury their anger deep inside their soul and then spend their lives wondering why they cannot find peace and joy. They go through life thinking that their anger is justified, but we can never justify what God condemns. I urge you to refuse to live your life angry. Why stay angry with someone who is enjoying life and perhaps doesn't know—or even care—that you are upset?

I wasted years hating my father for abusing me, and I say "wasted" because that is exactly what I did. All of my anger and hatred did not change a thing. It didn't change him, and it didn't change what happened. But it did change me in a very negative and nonproductive way. Being angry is like taking poison and hoping that it will kill your enemy. It only hurts you! Do yourself a favor and forgive. Your joy will return, and as you forgive and trust God to deal with the

> Being angry is like taking poison and hoping that it will kill your enemy. It only hurts you!

situation, you will see results. Our enemies cannot pay us back for what they have taken from us, but God can and will if we trust Him.

Learning to be merciful toward the faults of others releases joy in our lives. We can choose to confront every minor thing that someone does to distress us, or we can be merciful and understanding. There are things that we do need to confront, but a lot of things that we turn into huge problems could be easily overlooked if we would choose to be more merciful. I am very grateful that God doesn't make a big deal out of every little mistake that we make, aren't you? He does chastise us for our own good, but He doesn't overload us with excessive reminders of our flaws. If He did we would be overwhelmed and unable to press forward.

I believe that hidden sin dilutes our joy. We need to live in the light and be quick to repent and receive forgiveness. God knows everything about us anyway and the best thing for us to do is face our faults and ask God to help us. The psalmist David even asked God to clear him of unconscious faults (Psalm 19:12). He didn't want to have anything on his conscience, not even something he wasn't fully aware of. A guilty conscience is a heavy burden and definitely a joy stealer.

I could probably write an entire book on things that dilute our joy, but I encourage you to consider the things I have said, and then pray for God to show you anything else in your own life that might be diluting your joy. Refuse to live without joy. Jesus died that we might have and enjoy our lives in abundance and to the full (John 10:10). God is glad. He is not sad or mad and He wants us to live the same way. He has offered us eternal life and that means life as God lives it. "Rejoice in the Lord always. Again I will say, rejoice!" (Philippians 4:4 NKJV).

CHAPTER 11

Be the Person God Meant You to Be

To be yourself in a world that is constantly trying to make you something else is the great accomplishment.

Ralph Waldo Emerson

Being the person God meant you to be is necessary for your own fulfillment. God won't help you be someone else. He created each of us carefully and intricately with His own hand while we were in our mother's womb, and He doesn't make mistakes. I urge you to love and embrace yourself and never struggle trying to be something or someone that you are not.

I like what Oscar Wilde said: "Be yourself, because everyone else is already taken." If we try to be someone else, we are bound to be frustrated, because we are attempting the impossible. Although others may be an example to us, they are never meant to be our standard.

Self-Acceptance

Do you like yourself? Most people don't, you know. Some of them know they don't like themselves, while others don't even have a clue that self-rejection is the root of many of their problems. For example, if we don't get along with ourselves, we won't be able to get along with other people either. I had great difficulty in my first forty-five years of life maintaining peaceful, healthy relationships with people. I was a lonely teenager and young adult and never really felt that I fit in anywhere. My first marriage failed because I married someone who had more problems than I did, and all we did was give each other problems. He didn't know how to love me and I didn't know how to love him. He was unfaithful on numerous occasions and finally the relationship ended.

Fortunately, God sent Dave into my life when I was twenty-three years old, but I had lots of baggage that I had not unpacked yet, and Dave got more than he bargained for. But he allowed God to work through him so he could be a good example to me of the life I could have, a life of self-acceptance, peace and joy in Christ. Spend some time with yourself and take an inventory of how you feel about yourself. What kind of picture do you carry in your mind of yourself? Our self-image is like the photos we carry in our wallet. When you look at yourself, do you see someone who has no value, no particular talent or ability, nothing to offer to the world, someone unloved, unwanted and unnecessary? Do you feel that you have made too many mistakes and that it is just too late for you? Or do you see yourself recreated in Christ Jesus, a new creation with a new nature, the home of God, loved, created in God's image, forgiven and standing on the brink of an exciting and fulfilling future? You can choose what you believe! God sets before each of us life and death, good and evil, and gives us the responsibility of choosing which one we will pursue.

Growing up in an abusive and angry home, I lacked self-worth and confidence. I felt flawed and didn't love myself so I was unable to love anyone else properly. God's Word tells us to not merely desire peaceful relationships with God, ourselves and others, but to pursue and go after them (1 Peter 3:11). The word "pursue" means to go after passionately and purposefully. Are you passionate or passive?

Seek God and His will for you, and pursue peace with Him, yourself and other people. Pursue the knowledge of who you are in Him and your privileges as a child of God. It will be a lifetime pursuit, because we are always learning and understanding more deeply and clearly the mysteries of God. For me, the journey has become the most exciting part of my relationship with God. I love reaching my goals, but I am also always aware that as long as I live, there will always be new goals in front of me.

Receive and Give

As I seriously sought God's counsel about why I had such difficulty in relationships, He taught me that I could not give away what I did not have. I had not received God's unconditional love, so I could not give it to others. I had not received God's complete forgiveness, so I could not give it away to the people in my life who needed it.

I saw God as angry about something most of the time, and I was angry most of the time about something, too. I was angry with myself for my flaws and also angry with other people for theirs. I hadn't yet learned that our view of God affects our relationship with Him and all of our other relationships as well. We don't need to wait until we are perfect to receive God's love, and we must not demand perfection from others either. If we do, it will place a burden on them that they cannot bear, and it will destroy our relationships with them.

Freely you have received, freely give.

Matthew 10:8

Why do we find it so difficult to receive? I believe it is because we have a *"work and earn"* mind-set. Receiving something from God—or anyone else, for that matter—that we don't feel we have earned or deserve is something we must learn to do graciously and with thanksgiving. Salvation is a gift; it cannot be earned or deserved. It comes by God's amazing grace and is received through faith (simple trust and reliance on God).

> *For it is by free grace (God's unmerited favor) that you are saved (delivered from judgment and made partakers of Christ's salvation) through [your] faith. And this [salvation] is not of yourselves [of your own doing, it came not through your own striving], but it is the gift of God.*
>
> Ephesians 2:8

Just as we cannot earn salvation, we cannot earn any of the blessings of God. If we love God, we will strive to do what is right, not in order to get anything, but because of what we have been given freely by His grace.

Learn to receive freely all that God wants to give you. He desires to show His love for you in tangible ways. He will give you favor, open doors of opportunity for you, meet your needs and bless you in amazing ways. But if you cannot receive what He gives, you stop the process before it is completed. God is a giver, and we must receive from Him before we will have anything to give to others. I love the verse below and would ask that you take time to really think about what it is saying to you personally.

> *For out of His fullness (abundance) we have all received [all had a share and we were all supplied with] one grace after*

another and spiritual blessing upon spiritual blessing and even favor upon favor and gift [heaped] upon gift.

John 1:16

I told this story in my book *How to Succeed At Being Yourself,* but it is worth re-telling here:

A godly man told me that a very expensive automobile had been given to him. The man had been faithful in ministry for many years. He had worked hard and made many sacrifices. A group of businessmen who knew and appreciated him wanted to bless him with a certain automobile that they knew he admired but could never own without supernatural intervention.

The man told me that he was thinking about selling it. I asked him if that would offend or hurt the men who had given him the gift. He responded that they had told him he could do with it as he pleased. I recall asking him why he would sell it since it was something he had always wanted and God had obviously provided. I remember his exact words to me. He said, "I know that I shouldn't feel the way I do, but to tell you the absolute truth, I don't feel worthy to drive a car this expensive."

He was actually correct in saying he wasn't worthy because none of us are, and that is what makes God's goodness so amazing. Fortunately, we don't get from God what we deserve, but what He chooses to give, and we should learn to receive and be amazed and very thankful.

Although we cannot earn or deserve the good that God does for us, He does bless right action, but only when it is done with right motive. If we do good things in order to get something (to earn or deserve), then our motive is wrong. But if we do them because that is simply who we are, then it is pleasing and acceptable to God. Do all the good works that you can possibly do, but always remember that our motive for what we do is the most important thing to God. Don't do things to be seen and admired by men, or to feel good about yourself, but simply because as a child of God, you are a dispensary of good to all you come in contact with. We must remember that we would not even know what "good" is unless God revealed it to us. All good things come from God; there is no other source (James 1:17).

What Does Your Future Hold?

We would all like to know what the future holds for us, but we may not realize that how our future turns out is partially dependent on us. God does have a plan for each of us to have a good future, but we must learn to cooperate with His plan rather than doing things that thwart it. God wants us to live the good life that He has prearranged and made ready for us to live (Ephesians 2:10). We need to say along with the apostle Paul, "I press on to lay hold of (grasp) and make my own, that for which Christ Jesus (the Messiah) has laid hold of me and made me His own" (Philippians 3:12).

In order to press on we must forget what lies behind. Your future has no room in it for your past. Take the good things from the past that you have learned along with you, but let go of anything that is holding you back or keeping you stuck in fear or insecurity of any kind. Letting go isn't as difficult as you might think it is. Start by no longer thinking about the things that made you mad or upset, or your own failures that disappointed you. Don't talk about them anymore. The more we rehearse something, the more likely we are to keep doing it. As you change your mind and your conversation, your feelings will begin to change. You can have hope instead of hopelessness. Remember, no matter how many mistakes you have made in the past... GOD IS NOT MAD AT YOU!

Start today believing that your future is filled with good things and refuse to give up until you are enjoying all of them. Start today being the person God meant you to be!

Learn to Enjoy Yourself

You will never be able to be anyone but you, so you may as well start enjoying yourself. If you have a tendency to compare yourself with other people and then struggle trying to do what they do—I urge you to stop! I was miserable for years trying to be other people—my pastor's wife, my neighbor, my husband and many others. I didn't like or enjoy who I was, so I looked to others to tell me what I should be. Don't let other people make your decisions, because you alone will have to deal with the results of them. My well-meaning neighbor strongly urged me to learn to sew. She loved sewing and was sure I would love it, too. I took sewing lessons and bought a sewing machine, but I hated sewing. Watching me learn to sew was fulfilling to her, but it was torment for me.

I tried to pray like one woman I knew, follow the Bible study program of another, be sweet and gentle like another, and I even tried to have

> I tried to pray like one woman I knew, follow the Bible study program of another, be sweet and gentle like another, and I even tried to have a garden like one woman I knew. When I was exhausted emotionally from trying to be other people, I finally learned that God would only help me be me!

a garden like one woman I knew. When I was exhausted emotionally from trying to be other people, I finally learned that God would only help me be me! True, I wasn't like other people; I could not do all the things they could do, but I could do what I could do—and it was time to start doing it.

Never apologize for being the person you are. That would be like an apple tree apologizing for not being a banana tree. If you're an apple tree, then produce apples; if you're a banana tree, then produce bananas! It takes all kinds of fruit to make a fruit salad. My point is that God has created us all very different on purpose. Each of us is unique and we have something to offer. When each of us becomes the best we can at being ourselves, then God's purpose can be fulfilled.

> Never apologize for being the person you are. That would be like an apple tree apologizing for not being a banana tree. If you're an apple tree, then produce apples; if you're a banana tree, then produce bananas! It takes all kinds of fruit to make a fruit salad.

God is not upset about who you are. He created you and only expects you to be you. While it is true that we all do things we should not do and we need to improve, it is also true that we don't need to try to change who we are. Changing our behavior is something God will help us with, but as I said, He will not help us be someone else.

Run Your Race

Do you not know that in a race all the runners compete, but [only] one receives the prize? So run [your race] that you may lay hold [of the prize] and make it yours.

1 Corinthians 9:24

We are each encouraged to run our race, not someone else's. However, if we are trying to run someone else's race, then we are destined to lose. If we admire qualities in another person, we can ask God to help us develop those qualities, but even then they will flow out of us in a different way than they do in the person we admire. I know hundreds of Bible teachers and preachers of God's Word, but each of us delivers the Word in a different way. Some stress one thing and some another. They are all good, but all unique. An artist or a singer is the same way. Designers and decorators are all creative, but they create different things, and if they are wise, they can appreciate and celebrate the talent in others without trying to copy it.

I could have appreciated my neighbors' creative talents expressed in sewing, gardening and many other things without trying to copy them, but I didn't know that at the time. As long as we think we have no value and that something is wrong with us, we will struggle to be someone we are not, and we'll never have the joy of self-acceptance. Are you comparing yourself with others and trying to be who they are? If you are, this is the day to appreciate who they are and what they can do, but without competing with them in any way. It is time for you to be you!

> *. . . Let us run with patience the race that is set before us.*
>
> Hebrews 12:1 (KJV)

Growing into the fullness of the person God intends you to be will take time. You must run your race with patience, but you can enjoy each stage of your journey. You can enjoy yourself during each phase of growth and improvement. As long as you are pursuing God's perfect will for you, He is satisfied. It doesn't upset God if we have not arrived, but He does want us to press forward.

The Holy Spirit is our coach in life. As long as we run our race and not someone else's, He will always be running with us, giving us strength and ability for each step that we take.

Relax and enjoy yourself. Learn to give yourself permission to be a human being who is flawed. If we all learn to laugh at ourselves a little more, we will never run out of entertainment.

Stop Trying to Impress Yourself

I think a lot of our anguish over our flaws and weaknesses simply comes from trying to impress ourselves with our own perfection.

> *I think a lot of our anguish over our flaws and weaknesses simply comes from trying to impress ourselves with our own perfection.*

We desperately want to feel good about ourselves, but don't realize that we can feel good about ourselves even when we make mistakes, especially when we are sorry for them and want to improve. God sees your heart! He is more interested in you than in your performance. If you have children, you know that you didn't get angry with them if they fell down while trying to learn to walk, or if they spilled food on themselves while trying to learn to feed themselves. Not only did you not get angry with them, but you comforted them, encouraged them to try again and cleaned up any mess they made. God is the same way with us, and if we know that He isn't angry with us, then we don't need to be angry with ourselves either.

I need to tell you this, and hope that the news doesn't distress you too much, but you will always make mistakes as long as you are in a human body here on earth. The day will come when Jesus will return for us and then we will be perfected, but until then, thank God that He sent Jesus to stand in the midst of our weakness and give us His strength.

Because our self-image is so important, I want to end this chapter with a dozen truths for you to think about and begin to speak over your life. As you do, they will help remold your image of yourself, and you can begin to see yourself as God sees you.

1. I know God created me, and He loves me unconditionally.
2. I have faults and weaknesses, and I want to change. I believe God is working in my life. He is changing me daily. While He is working in me, I can still enjoy my life and myself.
3. Everyone has faults, so I am not a failure just because I am not perfect.
4. I am going to work with God to overcome my weaknesses, but I realize I will always have something to deal with; therefore I will not become discouraged when God convicts me of areas of my life that need improvement.
5. I want to make people happy and have them like me, but my sense of worth is not dependent upon what others think of me. Jesus has already affirmed my value by His willingness to die for me.
6. I will not be controlled by what other people think, say or do. Even if they totally reject me, I will survive. God has promised never to reject or condemn me as long as I believe in Him.
7. No matter how often I fail, I will not give up, because God is with me to strengthen and sustain me. He has promised never to leave me or forsake me (Hebrews 13:5).
8. I like myself. I do not like everything I do, and I want to change—but I refuse to reject myself.
9. I have right standing with God through Jesus Christ.

10. God has a good plan for my life. I am going to fulfill my destiny and be all I can be for His glory. I have God-given gifts and talents, and I intend to use them to help others.

11. I am nothing, and yet I am everything! In myself I am nothing, and yet in Jesus, I am everything I need to be.

12. I can do everything that God calls me to do, through His Son Jesus Christ (see Philippians 4:13).

CHAPTER 12

Developing Your Potential

Everyone has inside them a piece of good news. The good news is that you really don't know how great you can be, how much you can love, what you can accomplish and what your potential is.

Anne Frank

Anne Frank was a very young Jewish girl who experienced the invasion of Holland by Hitler. Jews were his target of destruction, and Anne and her family found a hiding place that they lived in for two years before being arrested. Anne was killed, but she had written a diary while in hiding that has inspired millions of people. While Anne was being daily threatened with capture and death, she was thinking of her potential. Surely, we have no excuse to not think about and develop ours.

I recall speaking to a young man on our staff who had great potential and yet had turned down two promotions that we offered him. I knew he had the potential, but that he was insecure and being held back by the fear of failure and a lack of confidence. He was trapped in his insecurities! He was doing his current job excellently and receiving a lot of encouragement from the people around him. He felt it was simply easier and more comfortable for him to remain where he was than to think of making a change. He preferred to feel safe with what he was familiar with rather than change, stepping out and risking failure. Nobody can develop their potential without making a few mistakes along the way, but if we know we are loved, that thought shouldn't frighten us. Although we may make mistakes, we will also have lots of success, and that is what we should focus on.

I talked with the young man and encouraged him. He said that he knew I was right and that he wanted to start stepping out. He had been asking God to let him do something new and different, and yet each time the opportunity came, he turned it down. Insecurity, self-doubt and fear can totally prevent us from reaching our potential.

One of the great tragedies in life is to not develop your potential. When you don't, you are robbing yourself and the world of your contribution. You might say, "Joyce, I have tried some things and failed, so now I am afraid." You can liberate yourself by realizing that your potential is not in your past. Any time we try and fail, we learn something that can benefit us in the future if we won't give up. The development of our potential requires patience and refusing to give up.

> *Any time we try and fail, we learn something that can benefit us in the future if we won't give up.*

The story surrounding the inventor of Jell-O is truly ironic. In 1897, Pearl Wait wore several hats. He was a construction worker who dabbled in patent medicines and sold his ailment remedies door-to-door. In the midst of his tinkering, he hit upon the idea of mixing fruit flavoring with granulated gelatin. His wife named it "Jell-O" and Wait had one more product to peddle. Unfortunately, sales weren't as strong as he'd hoped, so in 1899, Pearl Wait sold his Jell-O rights to Orator Woodward for $450. Woodward knew the value of marketing, so within just eight brief years, Wait's neighbor turned a $450 investment into a $1 million business. Today not a single relative of Pearl Wait's receives royalties from the 1.1 million boxes of Jell-O that are sold each day. Why? Because Wait just couldn't wait.

Only God knows how many amazing opportunities never came to fruition because of impatience. It is one thing to dream a dream, but dreams come to pass with much painful effort, sacrifice and patience. The thing that lies between potential and success is time. Pearl Wait had a product with potential, but he never succeeded because he wasn't patient. In our society today, when so many people are accustomed to instant gratification, we see less and less development of potential and creativity.

If you want to do anything amazing with your life, you will have to learn to work and wait! Developing our potential requires firm faith, not wishful thinking. When God gave me the opportunity to develop my communication potential by teaching His Word, I thought that I would be an overnight success. That of course did not happen, but what did happen were tiny bits of progress throughout many years of determination that eventually became an international ministry.

I had big dreams, and I believe that is good. What I did not have was an understanding of how long it would take to develop my dreams fully. Don't make small plans. I pray that you have a dream for something greater than what you have now, but I also pray that you can enjoy each step of your journey and that you will realize that success requires an investment of time and lots of hard work. Many people never fulfill their destiny because they are not willing to pay the price up front. They settle for something less than the best God has in His plan for them because they don't want to do hard things or take risks. I often say that in our society we are addicted to comfort and ease, and I believe that, but anyone can decide to swim upstream against the current of the culture they live in if they really want to.

Too many people take the "quick fix" method for everything. They want instant gratification and what makes them feel good right now. They are not willing to invest for the future. They will regret their decision eventually, because the future will come and it won't hold what they would have liked it to.

Millions of people daily look back on their lives and say, "I wish I had," or "I wish I hadn't," and all they have is regrets. I refuse to end up that way and I hope you will, too.

Don't Be Afraid to Try

God is amazingly creative and His Spirit dwells in us. We are created in His image, so that means we are creative, too. Think about how creative Adam had to be in order to name all of the animals in the Garden of Eden, and even after doing that, I am sure he had barely tapped into his God-given ability.

Do you live a life of boring sameness because you are afraid to try anything new? Do you assume you would fail without even trying? A great deal of creativity lies within each one of us, and we need to learn to tap into it and express it without fear. Often, instead of exercising creativity, we keep repeating the same things even when we are bored with them, simply because we are afraid to step out and do something different. Even if we feel safer and more comfortable with things we are familiar with, we still need variety in our lives.

God must be for variety or He would not have created so much of it. As we often hear, "Variety is the spice of life." Sometimes even a slight deviation from sameness is refreshing.

Some people keep the same job or live in the same area all of their lives because they feel those environments and activities are safe. Even if they hate their jobs and feel unfulfilled, at least they know how to do their jobs and are comfortable with them— the thought of getting a different job is terrifying to them! They think of all the negative things that could happen. "What if I leave my job and end up not doing well at the next one?" "I have friends where I work and I am accepted there. What if people at the new place don't like me?" "I would be lowest in seniority at a new place, so if there was a lay-off I would be the first to go." They think these types of things until they talk themselves out of making a change.

Bolder individuals who are determined to fulfill their potential think differently. They might think like this: "It will be exhilarating to do something fresh and new." "I need and want a new challenge." "I am excited about making new friends." "I believe I will make a contribution to the new company and quickly be promoted." We can talk ourselves into doing a thing or out of doing it, depending on our level of confidence. Fortunately, I have discovered that I don't have to *feel* confident in order to *be* confident. True confidence is found in Christ and not in ourselves. I know I can do nothing without Him, but I have learned to believe that I can do anything He leads me to do through Him.

I am not encouraging people to pursue every whim that crosses their mind or to latch on to every fad that comes their way. There is nothing wrong with having the same job all of your life if you are fulfilled in doing it and truly believe you are reaching your potential. If not, then I urge you to start praying and asking God to open new doors of opportunity for you, and when He does, then step out of your comfort zone—and into new things.

You Are Not a Failure Unless You Stop Trying

Failing at something does not make a person a failure. I had to learn that before I was able to keep pressing past mistakes and developing the potential inside me. Most of the people who have done great things or invented amazing things have failed many times before they actually succeeded. Abraham Lincoln said, "My great concern is not whether you have failed, but if you are content with your failure."

Why are we so afraid of not succeeding at something that we won't even try? I believe it is because of the fears we have about ourselves. Deep inside themselves, many people are desperately afraid that they are flawed and don't want to do anything that might cause those flaws to appear. I also believe that we care way too much about what other people think. We are never free until we have no need to impress other people. I also believe that being afraid that God will not be pleased with us if we fail keeps many people from stepping out.

> We are never free until we have no need to impress other people.

I personally believe that God admires boldness and courage. We must remember that He is the One Who told us in His Word not to be afraid of anything. Sometimes we are more likely to step out and try something if we don't know we can't do it. When God called me to teach His Word, I can truthfully say that I was not qualified and I had absolutely no knowledge of how to do it, but it didn't occur to me that I couldn't do it. I did not know I couldn't do it, so I did it. About two years after I started teaching my first Bible study, which was very successful, a group of more educated people said to me, "You can't do this; you are a woman, you're not educated, and you have had no training." It was too late for me to believe them, because I was already being successful at what they told me I couldn't do. Many people will tell you that you can't do a thing if it is something out of the ordinary, but if it is not ordinary, then it can be extraordinary.

> *Many people will tell you that you can't do a thing if it is something out of the ordinary, but if it is not ordinary, then it can be extraordinary.*

You Have What It Takes

Noah Webster's 1828 American dictionary of the English language defines *potential* in part as "existing in possibility, not in act." The fact that we have an ability does not mean that we will do what must be done in order to develop it. In other words, where there is potential, all the parts necessary for success are there, but they are not yet put into action. They still need something to propel them, something to empower and motivate them. They are often in embryonic form—they need to be developed. The person with the potential must make a decision to take action and not quit until he has succeeded. He must decide ahead of time that even if he fails twenty times, he will try again. He must be totally unwilling to merely exist without developing his potential.

It is good to be content. It is a godly quality, but we don't want to be so satisfied that we never want to see change. The best plan is to be happy where you are, while you're on your way to where you are going. Even in our relationship with God, we should always be hungry to know His Word more deeply and to know Him more intimately. Don't be satisfied with a mediocre marriage, but make the effort to make it the best it can be. To be mediocre is to be halfway between success and failure, and it is not the place God has ordained for His people.

I think there is so much mediocrity in the world today that we can easily sink into it without even realizing we have done it. I ask you to examine your life and your heart and see if you know deep inside that you are missing out on your best life. If you are, then it is time to make some decisions. You will also have to add effort and patience. There is a gold mine hidden in every life, but we have to dig to get to it. We must be willing to go beyond old mind-sets that hold us back. We need to go beyond how we feel or what is convenient. If we dig down deep enough, we will find God waiting to give us strength that we never knew we had. All He wants to see is some persistence and determination and He will partner with you in helping you be the best you can be.

You may look at the development of potential as something only for those who have some special talent, and you may not see yourself as being one of them. While it is true that people are gifted and talented in different ways, God's Word assures us that we all share in the gifts that God gives. You may not be a painter, singer, designer, speaker or author, but you are something. And whatever you are is important to God and to the rest of us. The Bible teaches us that even though our gifts vary like the various parts of our physical body, we are all mutually dependent on one another (Romans 12:4–5). Every person's part is a great contribution if he or she does it. A mother, a father, a teacher, a helper, an administrator, an organizer, an encourager or anything else is vitally necessary. You don't have to be someone else, but you do need to be "fully" you!

Don't Let Insecurity Hold You Back

"I'm insecure" can become an excuse to do nothing if we are not careful. The only way to conquer anything is to confront it. The best medicine for insecurity is to step out and try. Perhaps when I say that, fear strikes your heart. If so, it is a clear indication that you are just the one God is speaking to through me right now. Don't let fear steal your destiny. Satan uses fear to keep us from fulfilling our potential. I take the attitude that any time he tries to frighten me to keep me from doing something, then that is probably exactly what I need to do.

Perhaps you have been told in the past that you can't do things, so you stopped trying. But I am telling you that you can. Anything God leads us to do is something that we can do with His help. All things are possible with God! I despise fear, lack of confidence and insecurity because of what they steal from people. The world is filled with people who live unsatisfying lives due to these negative thought patterns and feelings they have about themselves. They may come from parents who did not do a good job raising them, or a teacher who wasn't kind, or peers who made fun of them, but no matter where they came from it is time for them to go.

It won't happen overnight or even because you read this book, but this can be a beginning. We never have an ending without a beginning, so let's begin. One of the things people who experience these types of problems need to do is to change how they think and talk about themselves. Don't say, "I am afraid," "I am insecure," or, "I have no confidence." Even if you feel that way, stop saying it! That alone will help you to get over your feelings. If a mind-set got us into a problem, then keeping the same mind-set won't get us out of it. We have to change our minds before we have any other change in life. One of the ways to renew your mind is to speak out loud what you want, not what you have. Yes, it is biblical! God calls things that are not yet in existence as if they already existed (Romans 4:17).

The next thing I suggest is stepping out in small ways at first, then, as you see that you survive trying little things, you will have more courage to do bigger things. When I started teaching God's Word, I did not start on a platform with twenty thousand people in front of me. I started with a small Bible study consisting of twelve women, and after a while that increased to twenty, and then thirty and eventually five hundred. Then I took other steps, and each one that I took frightened me, but I knew I had to try. I am sure you have heard the saying that "it is better to have tried and failed than never to have tried at all," and I agree with that. The only way to find out what you can and cannot do is to try some things, remembering that God loves you unconditionally and He will not get angry if you try some things that don't work while you are on your way to finding out what does work for you. Never forget that God does not expect us not to ever make mistakes. He is not angry with us when we do, but instead He is ever present to help us learn from those mistakes and recover with enthusiasm to try again.

Let me clarify that I am not suggesting that you try anything unless you believe that God is leading you to do so. He is the Author and Finisher of our faith, but He is not obligated to help us finish anything that He did not Author. If you have done all you can to determine whether or not you're being led by God and you still don't know for sure, then take a baby step forward and see if God blesses it. If He does, then take another step and another. If He doesn't, then at least you have stepped out and made an effort to find out.

Declare war on fear! Live boldly and courageously! Be determined from this day forward to fulfill your potential!

CHAPTER 13

Mercy Is Greater Than Anger

God's mercy is so great that you may sooner drain the sea
of its water, or deprive the sun of its light, or make space
too narrow, than diminish the great mercy of God.

C. H. Spurgeon

John Chrysostom, archbishop of Constantinople from 347 to 407, said, "Mercy imitates God, and disappoints Satan." When we receive mercy from God or extend mercy to others, it always disappoints Satan, because his goal is to keep us believing that God is angry with us and to make us angry with other people.

God is merciful! His mercy is great and it is new every day. His mercy is greater than His anger. You may recall that in the introduction to this book I said that God can and does get angry, but He is not an angry God. His wrath is against sin, but He extends mercy to sinners.

> *Return, faithless Israel, says the Lord, and I will not cause*
> *My countenance to fall and look in anger upon you, for I am*
> *merciful, says the Lord; I will not keep My anger forever.*
>
> Jeremiah 3:12

God's mercy cannot be grasped by our finite minds, but can only be received by the heart. In the chapters that follow, I intend to quote more Scripture than in earlier chapters, and I strongly urge you not to skip over them. Instead, read each Scripture slowly two times. In our thinking we want everything to be fair and just, but mercy is not fair. It goes beyond anything we can understand. So I ask you to read the Scriptures slowly, digest them and let them get into your spirit (heart). God will give us the faith to believe in mercy even though we may not understand it. There is no way to explain why a just and sinless God would decide to not punish those who deserve it, but instead give them grace, favor, blessing, forgiveness and love, all of which issue out of His mercy. But we can be grateful that He did!

> For His anger is but for a moment, but His favor is for a life-time or in His favor is life.
>
> Psalm 30:5

I want to repeat that God does get angry at sin, injustice and our foolishness, but His nature and character are not that of an angry God. Perhaps I can explain it this way. My father was an angry man and he quickly punished people for every tiny infraction of his rules. Being around him made my mother, brother and me fearful, nervous and tense, feeling guilty and condemned for something all of the time. Although we tried very hard to do what he wanted, it was impossible, because his rules were unending and they changed frequently. We lived in an atmosphere in which we constantly waited for punishment. My husband, Dave, is not an angry man. He can get angry if I do something really dumb or talk to him disrespectfully, but it only lasts for a moment. Dave knows my personality is a bit feisty at times and that I am sorry when I behave badly, so he extends mercy to me and is always willing to forget the misdeed and return to peace.

Dealing with an angry person is very different from dealing with someone who can get angry but has no desire to stay that way.

"God delights far more in His mercy than in His wrath," says Daniel Fuller in *The Unity of the Bible*. "So in order to show the priority of His mercy, He must place it against the backdrop of His wrath. How could God's mercy appear fully as His great mercy unless it was extended to people who were under His wrath and therefore could only ask for mercy? It would be impossible for them to share with God the delight He has in His mercy unless they saw clearly the awfulness of the almighty wrath from which His mercy delivers them."

We don't merely need mercy once in our life or occasionally, we need it frequently. Thank God His mercy is abundant and available at all times.

> *O give thanks to the Lord, for He is good; for His mercy and loving-kindness endure forever.*
>
> Psalm 136:1

Psalm 136 contains twenty-six verses, and each of them ends with, "for His mercy and loving-kindness endure forever." You and I can never do so much wrong that there is no more mercy left for us. Where sin does abound, grace (mercy) does much more abound (Romans 5:20). God is more willing to pardon than to punish.

> You and I can never do so much wrong that there is no more mercy left for us.

The following little story is a wonderful reminder of this.

One rainy afternoon a mother was driving along one of the main streets of town. Suddenly, her son Matthew spoke up from his relaxed position in the rear seat. "Mom, I'm thinking of something." This announcement usually meant he had been pondering some fact for a while and was now ready to expound all that his seven-year-old mind had discovered. His mother was eager to hear. "What are you thinking?" she asked. "The rain is like sin and the windshield wipers are like God, wiping our sins away." "That's really good, Matthew," she replied. But she became curious and wondered how far Matthew would take this revelation. So she asked, "Do you notice how the rain keeps on coming? What does that tell you?" Matthew didn't hesitate one moment with his answer, "We keep sinning, and God just keeps on forgiving us."

> *The Lord is gracious and full of compassion, slow to anger and abounding in mercy and loving-kindness.*
> *The Lord is good to all, and His tender mercies are over all His works [the entirety of things created].*
>
> Psalm 145:8–9

What Are You Looking At?

It is important to get our minds off the road behind us. When you're driving your car, what would happen if you spent as much time looking in the rearview mirror as you did looking at the road ahead? My guess is that you'd crash into something! There are times when it is appropriate to look back in life in order to assess what we've learned and use it to its best advantage. There are times when we enjoy looking back to reminisce. Experience is a good teacher, and looking back on it is wise. But if we look back too much, then we are not keeping our eyes on the road ahead.

By the same token, if we focus on our past errors, bad choices and mistakes, then we are dwelling in the past, which is usually not helpful in the present.

We each make mistakes, we fail, and we sin, but God's mercy

is new every day! Since mercy is a gift, it cannot be earned or deserved in any way; it may only be received by faith. In order to receive mercy for the things that are behind you (and any moment other than the one you are currently living in is behind you), you must get your mind off your past failure and onto Jesus. Paul teaches us in Hebrews that we are to look away from all that will distract us unto Jesus (Hebrews 12:2). When you pray do you fellowship with your sin or with Jesus? We can think so much about what we have done wrong that we fail to see the amazing mercy of God.

What we look at in our heart is very important. How much time do you spend meditating on and feeling bad about your faults, weaknesses, failures and sins? We should recognize them and repent (turn away from them), but when we turn away, we must turn to something else (Jesus), otherwise we will turn right back to them. Keep your thoughts on what Jesus did for you on the cross. God's mercy is greater than His wrath. God never stops loving us for one moment, not even when we do bad things. His mercy is offered in an effort to heal and restore us.

Looking back gives constant opportunity to return (Hebrews 11:15). The man ultimately follows where he allows his thoughts to go. God is not only merciful toward our sins, but He chooses to remember them no more (Hebrews 8:12). That clearly means that He wants us to do the same thing. There was a time in my life when if you had asked for a list of my recent sins, I could have easily rehearsed many of them from the mental list I kept. Now, if you asked me the same question, I might be able to tell you something that was very fresh, but I certainly could not give you a list, because I no longer keep one. When I sin and the Holy Spirit convicts me, I tell God I am sorry because I truly am, I receive His forgiveness and mercy, I ask Him to help me not to repeat the same mistake and I keep my eyes on the goodness of God and go on about the business of living life to the full.

If God had wanted us to be miserable, He would not have offered us mercy! We should definitely feel sorry for our sins. The apostle James even suggests that we should grieve over them (James 4:9), but he says in the very next verse that as we humble ourselves in God's presence, He will lift us up and make our lives significant. God does not want us to feel belittled and insignificant because we sin; He wants us to face our faults, receive mercy and press on.

> If God had wanted us to be miserable, He would not have offered us mercy!

> God does not want us to feel belittled and insignificant because we sin; He wants us to face our faults, receive mercy and press on.

A young mother recently told me that she spends most of her day being aware of her sins and trying to be sure she confesses each of them so she can come back into fellowship with God. She is focused on her sin. She is living under the law and is completely exhausted spiritually from her misunderstanding of God's ways. We should never be excessively introspective and obsessed with our every fault. Trust the Holy Spirit to convict and convince you of sin and righteousness. He shows us what we are doing wrong, and also shows us the right way to do things. He does not leave us struggling to try in our own strength to change our ways, but He gives us the grace (strength) to do them.

When Jesus ascended to heaven, He sent the Holy Spirit to be in close fellowship with us and said:

> *When He comes, He will convict and convince the world and bring demonstration to it about sin and about righteousness*

(uprightness of heart and right standing with God) and about judgment.

John 16:8

Please notice that the Holy Spirit does not only convict us of sin, but goes on to convince us of righteousness. We are in right standing with God through the blood of Jesus, and we must always remember that—especially when we sin. We don't lose our fellowship with God each time we make a mistake. He never leaves us or forsakes us, but He is with us always. The moment you are convicted of sin, turn to Jesus, because it is only His blood that saves us.

At the risk of being accused of heresy, let me say that I think we often are too preoccupied with our sin. Perhaps we make more of it than God does. He has already provided a solution for sin. Sin is not a problem for God because He is able to forgive it, forget it and offer mercy to the sin-ner. Sin is only a problem for us if we continue in it after having been shown the awfulness of it. If we will-fully refuse to turn away from it, then it will consume us. God's grace meets us where we are, but it never leaves us where it found us. So let go of what lies behind and move on!

> *Sin is not a problem for God because He is able to forgive it, forget it and offer mercy to the sinner. Sin is only a problem for us if we continue in it after having been shown the awfulness of it.*

The apostle Paul said something that indicates to me that sin can be more easily dealt with than we often imagine that it can.

My little children, I write you these things so that you may not violate God's law and sin. But if anyone should sin, we have an Advocate (One Who will intercede for us) with the Father—[it

*is] Jesus Christ [the all] righteous [upright, just, Who conforms
to the Father's will in every purpose, thought, and action].*

1 John 2:1

What a glorious Scripture verse this is! Of course our desire
should be to not sin, but if we do sin, God has already taken care
of it. We can look to Jesus, who has been and is perfect in our
place. He conforms to the Father's will perfectly in every area,
and He intercedes for us with God. God forgives us for Jesus'
sake. When we go to God in Jesus' name, then He sees Jesus, not
our sin. He will forever honor the sacrifice that Jesus made for us
in obedience to Him.

I cannot recall any of the heroes of the Bible, the men and
women we admire from the past, rehashing and discussing their
past sins. Paul mentioned his only for the purpose of explain-
ing how amazing God's grace is. Peter denied Christ three times,
and he went on to become one of the greatest apostles and never
mentioned his failure again. Abraham, Moses and Elijah all had
faults. Abraham lied because he was afraid, Moses had a bad temper, and Elijah was afraid of Jezebel and became depressed. Mary
called Magdalene had been a prostitute who had seven demons
cast out of her. God dealt with them regarding their sin, but in
the Bible, they never mention it again. Truly, in Christ we are new
creatures, old things pass away and all things become brand-new!

Elijah is used as an example of a man who had like nature as
we have (weak) and yet he prayed for it not to rain and no rain
fell on the earth for six months. Then he prayed again, this time
for rain, and the heavens supplied rain (James 5:17–18). Elijah's
weak human nature was only referenced to help us understand
that even though we are imperfect, we can still boldly approach
the throne of God and pray effective prayers.

I implore you to receive the great and abundant mercy of God, stop looking back and enjoy an effective partnership with God. He needs us to be strong in Him, not weak and ineffective in our sins and failures. God has much to do yet on the earth. And He intends to work through His people. Don't miss the part He wants you to do because you are so focused on the past that you miss what God has for you right now.

Are All Sins Equal?

One sin is as easy for God to forgive as another. All of our sins, past, present and future, were paid for when Jesus died on the cross. There is no sin so bad that God cannot forgive it completely, but not all sin is equal in regard to the effect it has on us, and our lives.

A person may lose her temper and say or do something she regrets; she can admit her failure, receive mercy and move on quickly. A person may commit adultery and destroy his family and still be just as easily forgiven, but it may take him more time to fully recover because of the damage that has been done not only to him, but to his family and others.

I readily admit that some things are easier to forget than others, so when I say we should stop looking at our sin, I do realize that time for healing is often necessary. If someone murders another person, he can receive forgiveness and mercy from God; but he may spend his life imprisoned and daily remember why he is confined to a cell. However, he can still recover spiritually, emotionally, and mentally. He can have an intimate relationship with God and even be used by Him while in prison.

> In fellowship with God, we daily look away from ourselves—and our sins—and look at Jesus.

In fellowship with God, we daily look away from ourselves—and our sins—and look at Jesus. A person may spend his life in prison for a crime he committed, and although he is in a physical prison, he can be spiritually, mentally and emotionally free through the grace, favor, love, forgiveness and mercy of God.

There are things I do wrong that I am convicted of and receive mercy for all in less than fifteen seconds. But occasionally there are things that I am convicted of, receive mercy for, but have to deal with in my soul for a few days. I believe there are times when God keeps the loving pressure that only He can apply on our souls for a period of time in order to impress on us the importance of a thing. If your child carelessly spills his milk each night at the dinner table, you might eventually take away his play privileges for a day in order to make your point that he needs to be more careful. But if he continually runs out into the street into oncoming traffic, you might take away his privileges for a month because the result of his error could be more devastating to him if he doesn't clearly understand and remember what you have told him. This is done out of the parents' love for the child and for no other reason.

God disciplines those whom He dearly and tenderly loves, and we should appreciate that and embrace it. Even though we may still feel the chastisement of God, that does not mean that we are not completely forgiven. It only means that God is doing a deeper work in us in order that we might not repeat the same errors. According to God's Word, we are destined to be molded into the image of Jesus Christ (Romans 8:29). If you were a piece of clay and a potter was molding you into a shape other than what you once were, I can assure you that it would not feel good and you would be tempted to resist it. When God is working to mold us into the image of Jesus, it usually doesn't feel good. It can hurt for much longer than we think we can endure, but God does know exactly what He is doing, and it will work out well in the end. The fact that we are still hurting does not mean that we are not forgiven. Pain doesn't mean that God is angry with us, or that He is punishing us. It just means that He is working and changing things for the better.

The shapeless, gray, cold piece of clay may resist being remolded by the potter and being placed into the baking ovens over and over again, but eventually it will be admired by many because it has become a fine piece of beautiful china, sought after by many.

Always cooperate with the work God is doing in you. The more we resist, the longer it takes. Don't ever let how you feel dictate God's love for you. He is always loving us, even when our circumstances don't make us feel good.

CHAPTER 14

Mercy Can Never Be Earned

Mercy can never be earned. Its very necessity is evoked by unworthiness, else there would be no need for it. Because we have sinned, we need mercy, not because we have obeyed.

Bob LaForge

Because our experience in life leads us to believe that we must earn and deserve any good thing we get, we often find it difficult to simply receive mercy. Mercy is outrageous! Who does something good for someone who is bad? God does! Instead of getting what we deserve as sinners, we are given the opportunity to stand forever in the presence of God. We are given right standing with God. He views us as being right instead of wrong!

John MacArthur reminds us "that even Jesus' most scathing denunciation—a blistering diatribe against the religious leaders of Jerusalem in Matthew 23—ends with Christ weeping over Jerusalem (v 37). Compassion colored everything He did."

Jesus seemed to be quite angry in His discourse recorded in Matthew, but it is quickly swallowed up by His compassion and mercy. Fortunately, the symbol of Christianity is the cross, not scales. God does not weigh

> *Fortunately, the symbol of Christianity is the cross, not scales. God does not weigh and measure all of our faults and charge us accordingly; He prefers to simply pay the bill Himself.*

and measure all of our faults and charge us accordingly; He prefers to simply pay the bill Himself.

> But God—so rich is He in His mercy! Because of and in order
> to satisfy the great and wonderful and intense love with
> which He loved us, even when we were dead (slain) by [our
> own] shortcomings and trespasses, He made us alive together
> in fellowship and in union with Christ; [He gave us the very
> life of Christ Himself, the same new life with which He quick-
> ened Him, for] it is by grace (His favor and mercy which you
> did not deserve) that you are saved (delivered from judgment
> and made partakers of Christ's salvation).

Ephesians 2:4–5

Now remember, I asked you to read these verses two times slowly and sincerely think about the beauty of what they are saying. God had to do what He did for us in order to satisfy His intense love. I have had occasion when love for one of my children has welled up in me with such intensity that I absolutely had to do something for them. You have probably experienced the same thing toward someone you love. If we can feel this way about flawed human beings, just try to imagine what God feels in His perfect love for us. He absolutely cannot leave us trapped in sin without providing an answer. He doesn't wait for us to deserve any benefit, but He rushes to the rescue because He cannot help Himself.

We are taught that in His love He chose us, made us holy, consecrated and blameless in His sight, and allows us to live before Him without reproach (any sense of guilt or shame). He does it for one reason only and that is because He wants to. It is His will to do so because it pleased Him and was His kind intention (Ephesians 1:4–5). Amazing! What can we say other than amazing!

I believe when we give mercy it increases our joy. It is an act of giving and the Word of God says that we will be blessed when we give to others.

As I said, mercy is absolutely outrageous. In *The Grace of Giving*, Dr. Stephen Olford tells a story that is a magnificent illustration of that.

> *In the days of the American revolutionary war there lived at Ephrata, Pennsylvania, a plain Baptist pastor, Peter Miller, who enjoyed the friendship of General Washington. There also dwelt in that town one Michael Wittman, an evil-minded man who did all in his power to abuse and oppose that pastor. But Michael Wittman was involved in treason and was arrested, and sentenced to death. The old preacher started out on foot and walked the whole seventy miles to Philadelphia that he might plead for that man's life. He was admitted into Washington's presence and begged for the life of the traitor. "No, Peter," said Washington. "I cannot grant you the life of your friend." "My friend," exclaimed the preacher, "he is the bitterest enemy I have!" "What?" cried Washington. "You have walked seventy miles to save the life of an enemy? That puts the matter in a different light. I will grant the pardon." And he did. And Peter Miller took Michael Wittman from the very shadow of death, back to his own home in Ephrata—but he went no longer as an enemy but as a friend.*

Miller's love demanded that an act that would normally have required justice be resolved by mercy instead. That is the way God deals with us.

In order to receive God's mercy, especially when we need it

daily, we must have a brand-new mind-set about how God deals with sin and sinners. First, He hates all sin, but He loves all sinners! God will never love you any more than He does at this moment in time, because His love is perfect at all times and is not based on anything that we do or don't do. No amount of improvement on our part can earn us any more of God's love. He has determined to give us mercy for our failures so we might continue to have fellowship with Him and receive the help from Him that we so desperately need. When we fail, we should never draw away from God, but we should run to Him, for He is our only hope of recovery from the error of our ways.

Grace takes the punishment that we deserve and mercy gives us blessings that we don't deserve. Can you receive it? Can you stand to be that blessed for no reason at all except that God is good?

The Whipping

There was a school with a class of students that no teacher had been able to handle. Two or three teachers had been run off from this school in one year by the unruly students. A young man, just out of college, heard about the class and applied to the school.

The principal asked the young man, "Do you know what you are asking for? No one else has been able to handle these students. You are just asking for a terrible beating."

After a few moments of silent prayer, the young man looked at the principal and said, "Sir, with your consent I accept the challenge. Just give me a trial."

The next morning the young man stood before the class. He said to the class, "Young people, I came here today to conduct school. But I realize I can't do it by myself. I must have your help."

One big boy, called Big Tom, in the back of the room whispered to his buddies, "I won't need any help. I can lick that little bird all by myself."

The young teacher told the class that if they were to have school, there would have to be some rules to go by. But he also added that he would allow the students to make up the rules and that he would list them on the blackboard.

This was certainly different, the students thought!

One young man suggested "NO STEALING."

Another one shouted, "BE ON TIME FOR CLASS."

Pretty soon they had ten rules listed on the board. The teacher then asked the class what the punishment should be for breaking these rules. "Rules are not good unless they are enforced," he said.

Someone in the class suggested that if the rules were broken, they should receive ten licks with a rod across their back with their coat off.

The teacher thought that this was pretty harsh, so he asked the class if they would stand by this punishment.

The class agreed. Everything went along pretty well for two or three days. Then Big Tom came in one day very upset. He declared that someone had stolen his lunch. After talking with the students, they came to the conclusion that little Timmy had stolen Big Tom's lunch. Someone had seen little Timmy with Big Tom's lunch!

The teacher called little Timmy up to the front of the room. Little Timmy admitted he had taken Big Tom's lunch.

So the teacher asked him, "Do you know the punishment?"

Little Timmy nodded that he did. "You must remove your coat," the teacher instructed.

The little fellow had come with a great big coat on. Little Timmy said to the teacher, "I am guilty and I am willing to take my punishment, but please don't make me take off my coat."

The teacher reminded little Timmy of the rules and punishments and again told him he must remove his coat and take his punishment like a man. The little fellow started to unbutton that old coat. As he did so, the teacher saw that he did not have a shirt on under the coat. And even worse, he saw a frail and bony frame hidden beneath that coat. The teacher asked little Timmy why he had come to school without a shirt on.

Little Timmy replied, "My daddy's dead and my mother is very poor. I don't have but one shirt, and my mother is washing it today. I wore my big brother's coat so that I could keep warm."

That young teacher stood and looked at the frail back with the spine protruding against the skin and the ribs sticking out. He wondered how he could lay a rod on that little back, without even a shirt on it.

Still, he knew he must enforce the punishment or the children would not obey the rules. So he drew back to strike little Timmy.

Just then Big Tom stood up and came down the aisle. He asked, "Is there anything that says that I can't take little Timmy's whipping for him?"

The teacher thought about it and agreed.

With that Big Tom ripped his coat off and stooped and stood over little Timmy at the desk. Hesitatingly, the teacher began to lay the rod on that big back.

But for some strange reason after only five licks that old rod just broke in half. The young teacher buried his face in his *hands and began to sob. He heard a commotion and looked up to find not even one dry eye in the room. Little Timmy had turned and grabbed Big Tom around the neck, apologizing to him for stealing his lunch. Little Timmy begged Big Tom to forgive him. He told Big Tom that he would love him till the day he died for taking his whipping for him.*

Aren't you glad that Jesus took our whipping for us? That He shed His precious blood on Calvary so that you and I can have eternal life with Him?

We are unworthy of the price He paid for us, but aren't you glad He loves us that much?

—Author unknown

God's Mercy and Our Mistakes

Many of our mistakes are made while we are trying to do something right. The apostle Paul said that although he wanted to do

> *Many of our mistakes are made while we are trying to do something right.*

right, he found that he kept doing wrong. He had the urge to do right, but no power to carry it out (Romans 7:18). We all experience that, and we must learn to receive mercy when we fail, look to Jesus and trust Him to continue working in us until our transformation is complete. In Romans 12 we learn that we are to be completely transformed by the entire renewal of our mind. We are made new creatures in Christ when we receive Him as our Savior and Lord, and we are daily learning to live according to the new nature we have been given. According to the apostle Paul's teaching, we must learn to "put on the new nature" (Ephesians 4:24). The simple truth is that God has done something wonderful in us, and we are learning to let Him work it out of us. Philippians 2:12–13 instructs us to work out our salvation with fear and trembling, being serious and cautious, and watchful against temptation. We cannot do it in our own strength, but we must let God work in us, and through us.

We may be sincere, but still be sincerely wrong. We may have good intentions, and still create a mess. God sees our heart, our motives and intentions and is willing to clean up our messes while we are growing. We never need to be afraid that God will get angry and give up on us, because He won't.

> *We may be sincere, but still be sincerely wrong. We may have good intentions, and still create a mess. God sees our heart, our motives and intentions and is willing to clean up our messes while we are growing.*

Six-year-old Brandon decided one Saturday morning to fix his parents pancakes. He found a big bowl and spoon, pulled a chair to the counter, opened the cupboard and pulled out the heavy flour canister, spilling it on the floor. He scooped some of the flour into the bowl with his hands, mixed in most of a cup of milk and added some sugar, leaving a floury trail on the floor, which by now had a few tracks left by his kitten. Brandon was covered with flour and getting frustrated. He wanted this to be something very good for Mom and Dad, but it was getting very bad. He didn't know what to do next, whether to put it all into the oven or on the stove (and he didn't know how the stove worked)! Suddenly he saw his kitten licking from the bowl of mix and reached to push her away, knocking the egg carton to the floor. Frantically, he tried to clean up this monumental mess but slipped on the eggs, getting his pajamas dirty. And just then he saw Dad standing at the door. Big crocodile tears welled up in Brandon's eyes. All he wanted to do was something good, but he'd made a terrible mess. He was sure a scolding was coming, maybe even a spanking. But his father just watched him. Then, walking through the mess, he picked up his crying son, hugged him and loved him, getting his own pajamas dirty in the process. That's how God deals with us. We try to do something good in life, but it turns into a mess. Our marriage gets all sticky or we insult a friend or we can't stand our job or our health goes sour. Sometimes we just stand there in tears because we can't think of anything else to do. That's when God picks us up and loves us and forgives us, even though some of our mess gets all over Him. But, just because we might mess up, we can't stop trying to "make pancakes," for God or for others. Sooner or later we'll get it right, and then they'll be glad we tried.

God's mercy sets us free to keep trying even though we often make messes. I recall some of the messes my girls made while trying to learn to bake, or to clean, or wear makeup. I recall our sons doing the same thing with other things. It seemed they were always wanting to borrow Dave's tools and not putting them back, or borrowing the car and returning it with the gas tank on empty. They were corrected, but loved and given mercy over and over again until they got it right.

> *God's mercy sets us free to keep trying even though we often make messes.*

Please don't have a wrong fear of God! Receive His mercy and let Him love you unconditionally. The more you do this, the more deeply you will fall in love with Him, and the next thing you know, you'll be obeying Him more and more with less effort than ever before. You will get it right if you just won't give up!

When Will We Get It All Right?

I tease Dave because no matter how good his golf score is after a round, he is never fully satisfied with his game. There is always something he feels he could have and should have done better. We are like that with life sometimes. Why can't we do it all right? It sure isn't because we don't want to. Before I had a serious relationship with God, I didn't care all that much how I behaved, but the more I learned to love Him, the more I wanted to do what was right all the time. However, it seemed that I made more mistakes than ever. I am sure I was making them all the time, but then I started noticing them, and not liking them. Even if I improved in one or two areas, there was always another about to be revealed to me that I hadn't seen before. People express this same frustration to me all the time. How can we passionately want to do good and still do wrong? Here is a Scripture to consider:

> For God has consigned (penned up) all men to disobedience, only that He may have mercy on them all [alike].
>
> Romans 11:32

Oh my, that seems rather unfair. No matter how hard we try, we are always going to have some flaws. Why? So God can display His amazing mercy in our lives. Experiencing the mercy of God draws us closer to Him. God makes sure that we always need Him. He leaves weaknesses in even the choicest of His saints to remind them that they still have need of Him. I think we must stop counting our mistakes! Don't keep score any longer. Why are we so obsessed with how much we do right and how much we do wrong? If God isn't counting, why are we? The score doesn't matter anyway, because if we do anything right God gets the glory for it, and if we do something wrong, only God can fix it, so whether we do right or wrong, we are "in Christ," and we belong to Him. Let's simply love Him as much as we can, do the best we can and trust Him to take care of all things. Be happy in God's love and acceptance, enjoy His mercy and forgiveness, grow in His grace and be delighted in His favor.

The apostle Paul was given two-thirds of what we read in the New Testament by direct revelation from God, and yet he had weaknesses that God refused to remove, but instead told him that His grace was sufficient for him (2 Corinthians 12:8–9). Paul said the weakness, or a thorn in his flesh, as he called it, was to keep him from being puffed up with pride over the greatness of the revelations he was being given. Once Paul heard this from God, he didn't seem to struggle any longer with the weakness. As a matter of fact, he said that he would glory in his weakness that God's power might rest upon him. He realized it was useless to fight with weakness that God was choosing to work through rather than to remove, and he simply entered God's rest concerning them. Can we do the same thing? I pray that we can.

Our temptation to become prideful is great as human beings, but nothing keeps us humble more than realizing that we make mistakes just like everyone else. One of the quickest ways to have one of your flaws show its ugly face is to judge someone else for his. We don't always understand the ways in which God deals with us, but we can be assured that His ways are perfect. When we truly want to be strong and we find ourselves being weak, we can trust God that His grace and mercy are sufficient for us. We might prefer to be strong on our own and not need God's help, but I have a feeling that if we could see everything God sees, we would realize that needing God's mercy is much better than not needing it at all.

Oh, the depth of the riches and wisdom and knowledge of God! How unfathomable (inscrutable, unsearchable) are His judgments (His decisions)! And how untraceable (mysterious, undiscoverable) are His ways (His methods, His paths)!

For who has known the mind of the Lord and who has understood His thoughts? . . .

Or who has first given God anything that he might be paid back or that he could claim a recompense?

For from Him and through Him and to Him are all things. [For all things originate with Him and come from Him; all things live through Him, and all things center in and tend to consummate and to end in Him.] To Him be glory forever! Amen (so be it).

Romans 11:33–36

CHAPTER 15

Amazing Grace

Grace is everything for nothing to those who don't deserve anything.

Author Unknown

When I think of the title *God Is Not Mad at You*, I hear the word "grace," and what a wonderful word to hear. If it were not for the grace of God, He would have to be mad at us, because His holiness demands justice for sin. A sacrifice must be made to atone for sin, but because of His grace, He made the sacrifice Himself by offering His Son's life for ours. Jesus took the punishment that we deserved for our sins, and offers to care for and bless us instead of giving us what we deserve. My friend, that is grace!

Martin Luther said, "Although out of pure grace God does not impute our sins to us, He nonetheless did not want to do this until complete and ample satisfaction of His law and His righteousness had been made. Since this was impossible for us, God ordained for us, in our place, One who took upon Himself all the punishment we deserve. He fulfilled the law for us. He averted the judgment of God from us, and appeased God's wrath. Grace, therefore, cost us nothing, but it cost Another much to get it for us. Grace was purchased with an incalculable, infinite treasure, the Son of God Himself."

Anger and the fear of it reduces us to downtrodden servants, but Jesus said, "I no longer call you servants…instead I have called you friends" (John 15:15). Only grace would allow us to be friends of God.

The Word (Christ) became flesh and dwelt among us. He was full of grace (favor, loving-kindness) and truth (John 1:14). It is by God's grace that we are saved through our faith; it is a gift of God, not of works, so that no man can boast or take credit to himself (Ephesians 2:8–9). The gift of God's grace is available to everyone. All we need to do is receive it by faith. Grace forgives our sins, cleanses us from all unrighteousness and places us in right standing with God. Truly amazing!

> [All] are justified and made upright and in right standing with God, freely and gratuitously by His grace (His unmerited favor and mercy), through the redemption which is [provided] in Christ Jesus.
>
> Romans 3:24

We could interpret Romans 3:24 to mean, "and God is not mad at you." We are invited into intimate relationship with God through Jesus Christ. He not only saves us, but He helps us with everything we need to do in life. The same grace that saved us empowers us to live in victory with peace and joy. In many of the apostle Paul's letters to the churches, he opens with the greeting, "Grace and peace be multiplied to you, from God our Father and our Lord Jesus Christ." It is impossible to have peace until we understand grace. Without grace we struggle and strive to earn or deserve what is already ours as a gift.

I like to use the example of trying to get into a chair we are already sitting in. Think of how ridiculous, frustrating and impossible that would be, and yet that is exactly what I did for many years, and perhaps you have also done the same thing. I continually tried to do right things so I could be right with God, but I was always disappointed and frustrated. I finally learned I could not "get" something I merely needed to "receive." How can we pay for something that is totally free?

Are You Trying to "Get" What You Should "Receive"?

"To get" means to obtain by effort, but "to receive" means to *simply* take in what is being offered. Our relationship with God and serving Him was never intended to be complicated. The apostle Paul told the people he ministered to that he was afraid that they would lose sight of the simplicity that was theirs in Christ Jesus, and we face the same danger. The world we live in today is very complicated, and it is not likely to change, so we must change our approach and keep our lives as simple as we possibly can. We should especially keep our relationship with God simple.

We can do that by believing His Word no matter what we think or how we feel. We can receive by faith all that He offers us, even though we know full well that we don't deserve it. We can be thankful for each favor that He gives us. We can choose to lean on, trust in and rely on Him to meet every need we have instead of worrying and trying to figure things out. And, with His help (grace) we can obey Him and grow in spiritual maturity knowing that His will and ways are always the best for us.

We often say that a person got saved. That is an inaccurate statement, because no one can "get" saved. Salvation is a gift that none of us can attain by our efforts. We don't "get" it, but we do "receive" it.

But to as many as did receive and welcome Him, He gave the authority (power, privilege, right) to become the children of God.

John 1:12

Some people feel that they must improve before they can have a relationship with God, but grace meets us where we are in our imperfect state and makes us what God wants us to be. Grace finds us where we are, but it never leaves us where it found us! Grace takes us the way we are! I like to say that when God invites us to His party, it is always a "come as you are" party. If a friend saw you outside your house raking leaves and stopped to say, "Hey, we are having a party at our house right now. Why don't you come on over?" you might answer, "I am not dressed for a party." But if your friend said, "We want you there, just come as you are," that would make you feel pretty special. That is in essence what God is saying to anyone who has not received Jesus as Savior yet. The good news is that you don't have to get fixed up before you can join God's party; you can come as you are.

Don't waste years of your life trying to improve before you enter into relationship with God. Jesus came to call sinners to repentance, not to call righteous ones. A physician does not attend to those who are healthy, but to those who are sick. Jesus came to solve the disease of sin. Answer the Lord's call. Come just as you are.

Wait and listen, everyone who is thirsty! Come to the waters; and he who has no money, come, buy and eat! Yes, come, buy [priceless, spiritual] wine and milk without money and without price [simply for the self-surrender that accepts the blessing].

Isaiah 55:1

Three times in this verse of Scripture we are invited to "come." The only thing we need to come with is an attitude of self-surrender. It is an attitude of "receiving," not one of "getting."

After Matthew had answered the Lord's call, he prepared a banquet that he might honor and entertain Jesus. He invited many publicans and sinners to come and eat with them. While they were at the table eating, certain Pharisees (religious people) and their scribes murmured. They could not understand why the Lord Jesus and His disciples would want to eat and drink with sinners! They complained to His disciples, saying, "Why do you eat and drink with the publicans and sinners?" The disciples could not answer, perhaps because they themselves did not understand why their Master would do such a thing. When Jesus heard about it, He replied, "I did not come to call the righteous, but sinners, to repentance" (Matthew 9:13 NKJV). That was His purpose for coming into the world. He didn't compromise Himself at all by eating with publicans and sinners, nor was He at the banquet by chance. He came with a definite aim.

Jesus did not expect the sinners to give Him anything, but He did come to give them everything, and it all started with His complete forgiveness and acceptance. He came to make a free offer and they only needed to receive. In the world, when we hear someone say, "This is free," we are usually suspicious that there is a hidden cost, but when Jesus says "free," He really means it.

Jesus said, "Freely (without pay) you have received, freely (without charge) give" (Matthew 10:8). When we learn to receive the grace of God freely, we are able to also give it away to other people. To receive grace (favor, mercy) from God is the first thing that we need to learn, and the second is that we should freely give it away to those in need. God never expects us to do for others what He is not willing to do for us. He shows us the way that we might follow His example. Do you desire to be more gracious to others? If so, then you must start by receiving abundant measures of God's grace daily for yourself.

Receive God's Word

Another thing we are to receive is the Word of God. Some hear the Word of God but don't receive it, and it does them no good. In Mark Chapter 4, we are told a parable of a sower who sowed seed (the Word of God) into different kinds of ground. The ground represented different kinds of hearers. I have learned that when I speak, not everyone hears the same thing. There are four kinds of hearers that are represented by the ground in this parable. The first is said to be ground along the path. The seed didn't go into the ground at all, and the birds came and ate it up. Some people don't want to hear at all. They have no interest in knowing truth, because they have no interest in changing. Even though their life might be miserable, they are not willing to make a change.

The second type of hearer we are told about is stony ground. The seed goes into this ground and immediately it is received, welcomed and accepted with joy, but it has no roots. When trouble or persecution comes, it is offended and falls away. The third type of hearer hears the Word, but the thorns—the cares and anxieties of the world, and the distractions of the age, and pleasure, glamour and deceitfulness of riches—prevent the seed from growing. We can see from this that even those who are willing to hear don't always hear fully, and in the right way. They don't hear with serious intent to truly *receive* the Word they hear. Only one hearer in this parable receives, welcomes and accepts it and bears fruit. God's desire is that we bear fruit. Many today hear and hear, but they are not truly listening. They may be sitting in a church pew, but they are not listening with spiritual ears. Casually listening to others share the truth of God's Word is like spraying a little perfume on yourself. You smell the fragrance, but in a short period of time the effect of it is totally gone. It is a temporary thing and has no lasting value.

When the Word of God is genuinely and sincerely received, it has the power in it to do an amazing work in our souls. It renews our mind and changes us into the image of Jesus Christ.

If you have been sitting in church for many years and have had no genuine change in your character, ask yourself if you are truly receiving the Word of God. If not, then all you need to do is start listening with a different attitude. Listen with an attitude of receiving and following through with action.

Receive the Holy Spirit

We are also instructed to receive the daily guidance of the Holy Spirit. When Jesus ascended to sit at the right hand of the Father, He sent the Holy Spirit to represent Him and act on His behalf. He is present in our lives to teach us, pray through us, convict us of sin and convince us of righteousness. He is present to lead and guide us in all matters of daily life, both spiritual and practical. I urge you to view the Holy Spirit as an ever-present help. He is referred to as "the Helper." Fortunately, Jesus did not leave us alone to fend for ourselves. I like to say that I am glad He didn't throw me the football (save me) and then tell me to try to make a touchdown by myself. He saves us by His grace and is an ever-present power in our lives, Who is available to all who will surrender and receive His help.

There are many other things we are told in God's Word to simply receive. They are forgiveness of sins, rewards, mercy for our failures, conviction of sin and guidance, just to name a few.

No matter what God desires to give us, it does not become ours unless we receive it. Don't ever waste effort trying to "get" what you can simply "receive" by faith. We must be baptized with a new way of thinking. Our mind must be completely renewed in order to enjoy the fullness of God's goodness in our lives.

Law and Grace Cannot Be Mixed

While the Law was given through Moses, grace (unearned, undeserved favor and spiritual blessing) and truth came through Jesus Christ.

John 1:17

Many new covenant believers still live under the old covenant, or they mix the old with the new. They have some grace and some law, but in reality they have neither one. The law demands that we work to keep it. It requires sacrifice on our part when we fail. The apostle Paul taught that works of the flesh and grace could not be mixed or both became useless. He said, "But if it is by grace (His unmerited favor and graciousness), it is no longer conditioned on works or anything men have done. Otherwise, grace would no longer be grace" (Romans 11:6). In order to have more clarity, we might say that grace is Jesus Christ working, and law is man working. God does not need our help to save us!

The law detects sin, but grace conquers it!

Saint Augustine

When we receive Christ as our Savior, we must put on a new garment (new nature), not merely sew new patches on the old garment. Jesus said that no man puts a piece of undressed (new) cloth on an old garment, for if he does, a worse tear is made (Matthew 9:16). We are already torn when we come to Christ. He doesn't wish to mend our old garment (our old way of life), but He wishes to do away with it and give us an entirely new one. He offers us a new covenant and a new way of living. We can live by faith, through which we receive God's grace, instead of living by trying to keep the law in order to soothe God's anger.

While it is true that God is angry about sin, we are told that Jesus "is the propitiation (the atoning sacrifice) for our sins" (1 John 2:2). Think of the bouquet of roses a man takes home to his wife to soothe her when she is angry with him for being late for dinner. He quietly walks in the door of their home holding the roses out in front of him. He knows she is very fond of roses and believes that the gift will pacify her anger.

Jesus is the offering to God that appeased His anger against all unrighteousness. When we go to our Father in Jesus' name, it is like holding out the roses in front of us and expecting them to make a way for us to be accepted. Jesus said, "No one comes to the Father except by (through) Me" (John 14:6). He is the Door through which we enter and find acceptance and love (John 10:9). A few good deeds done to cover up our sin are not enough. We must not sew new patches on old garments.

Imagine a woman wearing a dress that was five years old and had been laundered many times and is faded and worn. She tears the dress on Monday and takes a piece of new cloth, one that is bright in color, and sews it over the tear in the old faded dress. On Tuesday she has two tears and the does the same thing again. Now let's imagine she repeats the process every day for a month. How foolish would her garment look? We look that foolish when we try to improve our garment by sewing new patches on it instead of getting rid of the old and putting on the new.

Today we do not need to do anything except to confess that our garment is torn, that we are corrupted and are unable to do any good, and to ask Him to give us a new garment.

Jesus didn't come to add to the Law of Moses, but to fulfill it and give us a new and better way to approach God. He came with grace and truth. Some people think, "I am a sinner, therefore I must fast twice a week, give money and do good works and then I will be acceptable to God," but this is wrong. What the sinner must do is receive grace, forgiveness, favor and mercy as a gift and be thankful for it.

He can then learn to do good things, but he is no longer doing them to get God to love and accept him, but only because of the amazing grace he has freely received!

God is not for sale! He cannot be bought with good works of any kind. We must understand that our motives are extremely important to God. Yes, He does desire that we follow His example and do good things, but they absolutely must be done for the right reason. Any good work done to "get" something is ruined and has no value before God. Only works that are done because we have "received" something amazing are valuable.

God won't love the man who prays three hours each day and reads large portions of Scripture one bit more than He does the one who reads and prays less. The man might love and admire himself more, but God won't love him more! Once again, let me say clearly that God is not for sale!

In *No Wonder They Call Him Savior*, Max Lucado tells a moving story that I want to share with you.

Longing to leave her poor Brazilian neighborhood, Christina wanted to see the world. Discontent with a home having only a pallet on the floor, a washbasin, and a wood-burning stove, she dreamed of a better life in the city. One morning she slipped away, breaking her mother's heart. Knowing what life on the streets would be like for her young, attractive daughter, Maria hurriedly packed to go find her. On her way to the bus stop she entered a drugstore to get one last thing. Pictures. She sat in the photograph booth, closed the curtain, and spent all she could on pictures of herself. With her purse full of small black-and-white photos, she boarded the next bus to Rio De Janeiro. Maria knew Christina had no way of earning money. She also knew that her daughter was too stubborn to give up. When pride meets hunger, a human will do things that were before unthinkable. Knowing this, Maria began her search. Bars, hotels, nightclubs, any place with the reputation for streetwalkers, or prostitutes. She went to them all. And at each place she left her picture—taped on a bathroom mirror, tacked to a hotel bulletin board, fastened to a corner phone booth, and on the back of each photo she wrote a note. It wasn't too long before both the money and the pictures ran out, and Maria had to go home. The weary mother wept as the bus began its long journey back to her small village.

It was a few weeks later that young Christina descended the hotel stairs. Her young face was tired. Her brown eyes no longer danced with youth but spoke of pain and fear. Her laughter was broken. Her dream had become a nightmare. A thousand times over she had longed to trade these countless beds for her secure pallet. Yet the little village was, in too many ways, too far away. As she reached the bottom of the stairs, her eyes noticed a familiar face. She looked again, and there on the lobby mirror was a small picture of her mother. Christina's eyes burned and her throat tightened as she walked across the room and removed the small photo. Written on the back was this compelling invitation. "Whatever you have done, whatever you have become, it doesn't matter. Please come home." She did.

Christina did not have to buy her mother's love back with good deeds. She was not being asked to do anything except come home! Jesus' cry to the world is "Come home!" When I have been on a long journey, and especially if I have been in a foreign country where the customs and food are very different than my own, I am thrilled to come home. I can relax and rest at home in a way that is unlike any other place. When we come home to Jesus, He wants us to rest in His love, not be afraid He is angry with us because of the life we have lived in the past.

Before anything else, we must have this glorious foundation in our lives. We must fully understand that although the law is holy, it does not make a man holy, because the man cannot keep it. Although he might keep some of it, he will never be able to keep all of it, because man is weak and flawed. God did not give the law expecting man to keep it, but so that by trying to keep it and failing he might realize he needed a Savior. He sends the Lord Jesus as grace to the world.

CHAPTER 16

Greater Grace

For grace is given not because we have done good works,
but in order that we may be able to do them.

Saint Augustine

God gives us grace for salvation, but He doesn't stop there. Fortunately, He also gives us more grace so that we may do all that we need to do by it. One might say that the grace we receive for salvation is a grace for the spiritual matters in our life. It saves us, forgives us completely and gives us right standing with God. After salvation there are many practical issues to be dealt with, and God gives us more grace for all of them. Whether our needs are spiritual or practical, God's grace is always abundantly available.

As we learn God's Word, we will find in ourselves a desire to be obedient to what He asks us to do, and to stop doing what He doesn't want us to do. But we quickly find that no matter how hard we try, we cannot do it merely by decision or willpower. We fail miserably and feel frustrated because of our lack of ability to perform the good that we wish to do. God has given us a new set of desires, but it also seems that He has left us without the ability to perform them. Actually, He wants us to learn that He *is* our ability. He wants us to lean on Him for absolutely everything, including the ability to do things that He commands us to do. We must realize that God has commanded us, and only God can enable us.

I honestly believe that I might have died from frustration had I not learned about the "more grace" that is offered to us. Before I became serious about my relationship with God, I was not unhappy about my way of life, for I was unaware that I had as many problems as I did. I thought that everyone else had problems and that they needed to change so I could be happy and comfortable. However, studying God's Word quickly taught me that I had problems and that I was the one who needed to change. I wanted to change because I loved God. I knew that He loved me, but now I wanted to love Him. I saw that Jesus had said, "If you [really] love Me, you will keep (obey) My command" (John 14:15).

I tried everything I could possibly try in order to change myself, but nothing I did worked. If anything, I behaved worse instead of better. I was focusing on all the things that were wrong with me and did not realize that what we focus on becomes larger and soon it is all that we can see. I cried with the apostle Paul, "Oh unhappy and pitiable and wretched man that I am! Who will release and deliver me from [the shackles of] this body of death?" (Romans 7:24). My heart was right before God, I wanted to do the right thing, but my body (soul) was giving me trouble. After much suffering I finally saw what the apostle Paul did when he said of his own deliverance—"O thank God!...through Jesus Christ (the Anointed One) our Lord!" (Romans 7:25). When I saw that only Jesus could deliver me and that I did not have to struggle to deliver myself, I felt as if a ton of weight had been lifted from my shoulders.

Over a period of time, I began to encounter a number of

Scriptures that taught me that only grace could change my behavior. When we try to save ourselves, it is unacceptable to God and does not work; when we try to change ourselves it is the same way. We do need to change, but we must ask God to change us. We must lean on and rely on Him for all things in us that need to change. He does change us little by little, and the main instruments He uses are His Word and the Holy Spirit.

> *He gives us more and more grace (power of the Holy Spirit, to meet this evil tendency and all others fully).*
>
> James 4:6

Vine's Complete Expositionary Dictionary of Old and New Testament Words says this about James 4:6: " 'But He giveth more grace' (Greek, 'a greater grace'). 'God will give even a greater grace,' namely, all that follows from humbleness and from turning away from the world." Our part in this is to make the decision to humble ourselves and turn away from the world; God's part is to provide the power (grace) to enable us to do it.

The apostle James is speaking of believers who are like unfaithful wives, having an illicit love affair with the world. He states that the Holy Spirit Who dwells in us yearns to be welcome in all areas of our lives. He is filled with a divine jealousy for our full attention and commitment. James goes on to say that the Holy Spirit gives us more grace (a greater grace) to overcome this evil tendency and all others fully. How wonderful it is to know that God gives the power to meet all of our evil tendencies, no matter what they are or how often they appear. Believing this truth gives us the freedom to live without the fear of being rejected by God because of our weaknesses.

Grace Is Power

We hear that grace is undeserved favor, and it definitely is. It is unde-served favor manifested in power that enables us to do what we need to do in this life. I like to define grace like this: *Grace is the power of the Holy Spirit offered to us free of charge, enabling us to do with ease what we could not do alone with any amount of struggle and effort.*

Sanctification

Sanctification is the separation of the believers from evil things and ways. Spiritually we are sanctified (made holy) when we are born again, but practically, this is worked out in our life little by little through our partnership with the Holy Spirit. The Holy Spirit is the agent in sanctification. We enter this relationship with God by faith in Christ. Sanctification is God's will and His purpose in calling us. It must be learned from God, as He teaches it through His Word, and must be pursued by the believer ear-nestly and steadfastly.

"Although we are spiritually and legally made Holy at the New Birth in Christ, Holy Character is not vicarious," says *Vine's Complete Expositionary Dictionary of Old and New Testament Words.* "It cannot be transferred or imputed, but it must be built up little by little as the result of obeying the Word of God, and following the example of Christ in the power of the Holy Spirit. The Holy Spirit is the Agent in sanctification."

This definition of sanctification is very important for us to understand, so I will put it in my own words in an effort to make it even plainer: When we are born again through faith in Jesus Christ, God gives us a new nature. He makes us holy inside, but this holiness must be worked into our character. This is a process that takes place little by little as we study God's Word and learn to lean on the Holy Spirit (grace).

If I had a shirt with a huge stain on it and I washed it in laundry detergent, I might say that the detergent mixed with water was the agent that got it clean. In the same way, God's Word and His Holy Spirit remove the stains from our behavior. It is done by His grace but is chosen by us.

> ...Work out (cultivate, carry out to the goal, and fully complete) your own salvation with reverence and awe and trembling (self-distrust, with serious caution, tenderness of conscience, watchfulness against temptation, timidly shrinking from whatever might offend God and discredit the name of Christ).
>
> [Not in your own strength] for it is God Who is all the while effectually at work in you [energizing and creating in you the power and desire], both to will and to work for His good pleasure and satisfaction and delight.
>
> Philippians 2:12–13

When Jesus ascended to sit at His Father's right hand until His enemies are made a footstool for His feet, He knew we would need power to live the life He had died to provide. So He sent us that power in the Holy Spirit. However, just as we had to learn to lean on Jesus for salvation, we must now learn to lean on the Holy Spirit, Who is the Spirit of grace for all other things that we need in life. As we passionately pursue God's holy character, He provides the strength and ability for change.

Let's say that I go to church on Sunday where I hear a rousing sermon on being kind to my enemies. Now it happens that a friend has recently hurt my feelings quite deeply and I must admit that I have no natural desire to be kind to her. But because of my love for God, I want to do it in obedience to Him. If I merely go home and try to be kind, I will fail miserably. But if I go home telling God that I am willing, but cannot do it without His help, I will find that when I see my friend, God will indeed help me. I am thankful to Him, because I know that by myself I would have failed. I have a victory, but God gets the credit.

Change That Never Ends

The process of sanctification is one that never completely reaches an end until God calls us from this world and completely transforms us. Until then, we keep growing, and that is all that God requires of us. He wants us to desire His will and work with His Holy Spirit toward acquiring it. As *Vine's Complete Expositionary Dictionary of Old and New Testament Words* says, it is a holiness that is built up little by little through obedience to God's Word.

We must learn that God is not angry because we have not arrived at our desired destination of complete holy character. He is satisfied to find us daily pressing on toward the mark of perfection. When we believe this, it eliminates pressure from our lives. I find joy in saying, "I'm growing. I am not where I need to be, but thank God I am not where I used to be—I am okay and I am on my way!"

When I began studying God's Word over thirty years ago, I thought, "How can one person need as much change as I do?" Now, after all these years I wonder, "How can one person have changed so much?" But I also wonder if the process is ever done, because I still need changing every day. Thirty years ago that frustrated me, but today it doesn't disturb me at all. I thank God for what He shows me; I receive it as loving chastisement from Him and trust Him to change me in His way and timing.

God's Toolbox

What does God use to change us? He uses His Holy Spirit, the Spirit of grace. He also uses His Word, and our experiences in life (Proverbs 3:13). Each of these is equally important, and they all work together to mold us into the image of Jesus Christ. I have found that when I ask God to help me to love people unconditionally, I can expect to run into people who are difficult to love. This is God's way of providing me practice. If I pray for patience, I will get trials. If I pray to give more, God will ask me for something I want to keep. If I pray to be less selfish, I find that things in life don't go my way or as I had planned. God says that we will be "transformed" into the image of Christ. He did not say that we would say a prayer and get translated into His image. It is a process and God uses many tools while He is working His complete and perfect will in us.

Most of us spend many years fighting this process and searching for a less painful path, but there are no padded crosses in life. The cross without pain doesn't exist. We are to take up (receive) our cross, and follow Jesus' example (Mark 8:34). To me this simply means that I am to embrace the experiences that God sends my way in life and believe that as I apply His Word and principles, they will work good in me. When doing the right thing is difficult for us, we can say, "The discomfort I feel means that I am growing spiritually." When we apply God's Word in a difficult circumstance in life and it is easy for us to do so, that means that we have already grown spiritually strong in that area. There are things that were once very difficult for me to go through and remain emotionally stable that are currently not difficult at all, and there are other things that are still quite challenging for me. This helps me locate the areas in which I still need to learn and grow.

Learning to trust God's method is an important part of navigating the changes in our lives. My newest favorite scripture is:

He trusted [Himself and everything] to Him Who judges fairly.
1 Peter 2:23

When Jesus was reviled and insulted, He did not offer insult in return. When He was abused and suffered, He made no threats of vengeance. Instead, He trusted Himself and everything to God. What a beautiful picture of resting in God in the midst of the circumstances that life brought Him.

This, too, is my goal! I want to remain the same—as Jesus did—no matter what people do or what my circumstances are. I have come a long way and I have a long way to go, but at least I have a goal!

When Judas betrayed Jesus, Jesus didn't change. When Peter denied Him, He didn't change. When His disciples disappointed Him, He didn't change. He remained stable while the storms of life raged on, and His example has changed the world and continues changing it every day.

Let us pursue this kind of holy stability, asking God to mold us into the image of Jesus Christ!

There Is No Power Shortage in Heaven

God never runs out of power. As long as we keep receiving it, He keeps pouring it out. The apostle John exhorts us to abide in

Christ. To live, dwell and remain in Him. Apart from Him we can do nothing (John 15:5). Let us believe it and act accordingly. Our spirit of independence causes us a great deal of trouble and delay in life. The sooner we lean on God, the quicker we get the help we need. He says, "You do not have, because you do not ask" (James 4:2). It is only pride that makes it so difficult to simply say, "God, I cannot do this without You. Please help me!" We have some desperate need to do it ourselves so we can take credit, but God will not allow it. Fight as we may and struggle all we want, but God will prevail in the end.

There was something I asked Dave to do several times and each time he said he didn't want to do it. I eventually prayed about it and left it in God's hands, and just recently noticed Dave doing the thing I had not been able to get him to do. God's influence over people is always more effective than ours. When you want to see something change in another person, pray about it and know that God will be more successful than you ever could have been. God's grace made the change in Dave that I could not make!

We can have grace, and we can have more grace (greater grace). Receive all the grace you possibly can, and you will have still only used enough to equal one drop of the ocean.

I recently had a terrible cold and cough, and my doctor sent some cough medicine with the instructions to take daily as needed. I could not take enough cough medicine to take care of tomorrow's cough—I had to take it daily! We must take grace the same way. You may have something looming in the future that frightens and overwhelms you, and you feel totally inadequate to face it. We all have things like that in life, and truthfully today we are not ready to handle them. But when tomorrow comes, we will have the grace we need to do whatever we need to do. Believing that allows us to enjoy today without dreading tomorrow! I don't know what tomorrow may bring, but I do know from God's Word and life's experiences that I will have enough grace to enable me to handle it successfully, and so will you. Remember, "Grace is God's power available to you free of charge, enabling you to do with ease what you could not do on your own with any amount of struggle and effort." Start living in the grace of God and enjoying every second of your life!!

> *Grace is the incomprehensible fact that God is well pleased with a man, and that a man may rejoice in God.*
>
> Karl Barth

CHAPTER 17

Run to God, Not from Him!

The name of the Lord is a strong tower; the righteous run to it and are safe.

Proverbs 18:10 (NKJV)

Fear of anger causes us to run from the one we imagine is angry with us. It puts a wall of separation between us, but God never says, "Run from Me"; He always says, "Come to Me." How glorious is that invitation? The God of the Universe, the Almighty, the Beginning and the End, the Author and the Finisher of all things gives an invitation to all . . . "Come to Me."

Whatever condition you may find yourself in today or any other day of your life, God's invitation is "Come!" His invitation does not require us to be in any particular condition to meet with Him. If we have been good or bad, happy or sad, glad or mad, the invitation is still simply "come." We can come as often as we desire, and we will never find the door closed or God not at home. Fortunately, when we call Him, His line is never busy.

I was afraid of my father's anger during my childhood, and I remember hiding from him any time that I could. I purposely avoided being in the same room with him whenever possible. His presence made me tense and uncomfortable and I hated that feeling. I could not relax or enjoy anything. When I had a need, I always asked my mother for help instead of my dad, or I tried to take care of it myself before going to my dad. I even did without many things rather than ask for his help. Fortunately, our heavenly Father is not like many earthly fathers or other people that we deal with in life. He is always ready to help all of those who will simply "come."

Are you doing without things that you need and desire because you are afraid to draw near to God and simply ask for His help? Perhaps you feel that you don't deserve His help, and the truth is that you don't. None of us do, but He offers it anyway. He helps us because He is good, not because we are good.

> Perhaps you feel that you don't deserve His help, and the truth is that you don't. None of us do, but He offers it anyway.

When a child is hurt, the first thing he does is run to Mom or Dad as fast as he can, and if he can't run, he cries until help comes. A child doesn't worry about the last time he was bad, or whether he deserves Mom and Dad's help. He just has a need and automatically runs to the one who can meet it. We should learn to be the same way. A child who has a good relationship with his parents never outgrows this desire to run to Mom or Dad when life hurts. My grown children, who range in age from thirty-two to forty-six years, still do it, and I am honored that they do. Could you imagine saying to one of your children, "Don't run to me when you're hurting. I am mad at you because you haven't been good." That sounds ridiculous and we know we would never do that, so how can we ever think that God would?

Jesus said, "If any man is thirsty, let him come to Me and drink!" (John 7:37). What an open invitation! If we have any need, we may simply come to Him and have our thirst quenched. It seems that the only requirement for approaching God is to be needy. Jesus promises to never cast out anyone who comes to Him.

All whom my Father gives (entrusts) to Me will come to Me;
and the one who comes to Me I will most certainly not cast out
[I will never, no never, reject one of them who comes to Me].

John 6:37

Wow! How different my life would have been had I been able to have that confidence in my earthly father. I did not have that privilege, just as many of you did not, but fortunately, we have a Father we can go to now with the promise of never being rejected. A Father Who is far better than even the best earthly father in the world.

Are You Tired and Weary?

Life is not always as kind to us as we would like it to be. People hurt us, circumstances disappoint us and until we learn how to enter God's rest, we frequently feel weary. Here is an open invitation from Jesus:

Come to Me, all you who labor and are heavy-laden and overburdened, and I will cause you to rest. [I will ease and relieve and refresh your souls.]

Matthew 11:28

Anyone may simply come. To do so requires no special talent. We just need to be ready to say we need help and then humble ourselves and come to God's throne of grace and receive by faith the help and comfort that we need.

Jesus goes on to say in succeeding verses that He is humble, gentle, meek and lowly; not harsh or hard or sharp or pressing.

He is making sure that we understand His nature. He is a Helper who delights in lifting His people up. When the prodigal son returned home in Luke 15, his father was delighted. He had no attitude of "I told you so." He didn't say, "I knew you would waste your fortune and come crawling back to me for help." Rather, he saw his son a long way off and ran to him. I love the mental picture this story provides.

The son decided to come home to his father, and when he did he was met with favor and unprecedented goodness. His father embraced him and kissed him. He ordered that the best robe be brought for his son. In fact, it was the festive robe of honor that was put on him. He received a ring, sandals and a feast.

It would seem that the prodigal who wasted his father's money and embarrassed him by living a sinful life deserved punishment, not a party, but God is good even when we are not!

> *Mercy gave the prodigal son a second chance, grace gave him a feast!*
>
> Max Lucado

Perhaps you walked away from God at some time in your life and even though you have come back, you have never been totally comfortable. You wonder if God is angry with you, and that fear keeps you from totally entering into His presence and living the life He wants you to live. If so, then please believe that you don't have to sacrifice your future in order to pay for your past! Jesus has already paid, and it was payment in full. There is

> There is no fee that you have to pay to go to God's party. After all, it is being given in your honor, so it would be a shame if you didn't show up.

no fee that you have to pay to go to God's party. After all, it is being given in your honor, so it would be a shame if you didn't show up.

Close your eyes for a moment and imagine the words stamped largely across your life: PAID IN FULL. God's Word tells us that we have been bought with a price, with the precious blood of Christ. We owe no debt because all of our sins have been paid for, past, present and future. It feels good to not be in debt! Go ahead and feel the freedom...no debt! Does it seem too good to be true? Of course it does, but I urge you to believe it anyway. Take God at His word and enjoy His presence.

I am sure the prodigal son was humbled by his father's extreme goodness, but he did receive it and he enjoyed it. It would have made his father sad had he refused to accept his goodness. Love always wants to give and can only be satisfied by having someone who is willing to receive! Ask and receive that your joy may be full (John 16:24).

When we learn to come to Jesus, we can also learn to live a life of rest instead of weariness and struggle. We come to Him in faith, believing that His promises are true and it is the open door to entering His rest.

> For we who have believed (adhered to and trusted in and relied on God) do enter that rest.
>
> Hebrews 4:3

God's rest is not a rest *from* work, but *in* work. It is a rest that we live with as we tend to the duties of life. We trust, we don't worry; we are not anxious, we cast our care and we wait on God. We do what we can do, but we never try to do what we cannot do, for that is what wears us out. It isn't that we are not tempted to try to do such things, but we choose not to. We eventually learn to take life one day at a time, and we partner with the Holy Spirit in living each day fully.

Have you entered God's rest? If not, all you have to do is "come," and like a small child, simply believe!

Draw Near

God often says the same thing in a couple of different ways just to make sure we understand it. He gives the invitation to "come," and He also invites us to "draw near." I suppose we could come and still stand off at a distance, but to draw near speaks of intimacy, and that is God's will for us in our relationship with Him.

We have a High Priest who understands our weaknesses. Jesus was tempted in all respects as we are, and although He never sinned, He does understand (Hebrews 4:15). He understands and He gives an invitation to draw near.

> Let us then fearlessly and confidently and boldly draw near to the throne of grace (the throne of God's unmerited favor to us sinners), that we may receive mercy [for our failures] and find grace to help in good time for every need [appropriate help and well-timed help, coming just when we need it].
>
> Hebrews 4:16

We can see from this single Scripture that it is God's will that we fearlessly run to Him, not from Him. Distance is a relationship killer. We weren't made to serve the Lord cowering in the distance; we were made to live in a love relationship with Him. Up close and personal!

The invitation is for us to "draw near." The way has been opened up for us to go in and out freely.

> *In Whom, because of our faith in Him, we dare to have the boldness (courage and confidence) of free access (an unreserved approach to God with freedom and without fear).*
>
> Ephesians 3:12

St. Augustine said, "Remember this. When people choose to withdraw far from a fire, the fire continues to give warmth, but they grow cold. When people choose to withdraw far from light, the light continues to be bright in itself, but they are in darkness. This is also the case when people withdraw from God."

I believe that many people are desperate for the message in this book. They want to believe that God is not mad at them and they are welcome to draw near. An anecdote from Ernest Hemingway's short story "The Capital of the World" drives the point home.

> *A father and his teenage son's relationship had become strained to the point of breaking. Finally the son ran away from home. His father, however, began a journey in search of his rebellious son. Finally, in Madrid, in a last desperate effort to find him, the father put an ad in the newspaper. The ad read: "DEAR PACO, MEET ME IN FRONT OF THE NEWSPAPER OFFICE AT NOON. ALL IS FORGIVEN. I LOVE YOU. YOUR FATHER."*
>
> *The next day at noon in front of the newspaper office, 800 "Pacos" showed up!*

There are countless people who desperately want to know that God is not mad at them and that all is forgiven. God cannot do anything else other than what He has already done. We must now take Him up on His kind invitation to "draw near" and receive the help and healing that we need. The fire of God's love will always burn brightly, but it is up to us whether we are warm or cold. "Come," and warm yourself by the fire of God's unconditional love.

Fear Causes Retreat

There are those who draw back and remain in eternal misery because they don't believe that they can draw near. I was one of those people for a long time. Daily, something would separate me from God, but it was deception on my part that allowed it to be that way. God's invitation was open for me to draw near, yet I drew back due to fear of facing Him as I was. The awareness of our imperfections causes us to draw back.

Dave and I have four grown children and at different times each of them has pondered why it is still so important to them even as adults that they please us. I have watched one son plan a trip for us and be a little nervous the entire trip that something wouldn't go right for me and his dad and that we would be disappointed in him. It took years to convince him that all we expected was for him to do his best and that if something went wrong, we would not get angry with him.

One of my daughters has discussed with me her need for our approval even though she is a grown woman with children of her own. I think it is a very natural thing to want to please your parents. I found myself trying to do it as a sixty-year-old woman, and my parents and I didn't even have a close relationship. My mom is in a nursing home and I take care of her, but I have found that when she is unhappy about anything, I have to resist thinking that I need to keep her happy all the time. I am committed to meeting her valid needs, but her joy is her responsibility, not mine. I know that I don't need her approval, but something in me still wants it. If we feel that way with imperfect parents, how much more will we feel that way with God? We want to please Him. We want His approval and we must understand that we have it as a gift through our faith in Jesus Christ.

If we continue trying to earn God's approval by our own deeds of goodness, we will always have something separating us from Him. But if we come to Him by faith alone, trusting in His goodness, then we find an open-door policy and the freedom to enter in at any time.

I keep a sign sitting on a table in my office that says in big bold letters, BELIEVE. I do it to remind myself that is what God wants from me. He wants me to trust Him, place my faith in Him, and believe His Word. When we wholeheartedly believe, it leads us to obedience.

You might say that the password into God's presence is I BELIEVE. Don't let the fear of your own imperfections keep you out of God's presence any longer. Run to Him, not away from Him. He has everything we need and offers it freely to those who will "come."

CHAPTER 18

What Shall We Do About Sin?

It is impossible for a man to be set free from sin before he hates it.

Ignatius

Although we know that all manner of sin can be forgiven and there is no amount of sin that can prevent us from having a wonderful relationship with God, we do still have to deal with our sin. What shall we do about it? What should our attitude be toward it? I believe we must hate it just as God does, and that we must resist it steadfastly in the power of the Holy Spirit. We cannot be filled with God's Spirit and ever be satisfied with a life of sin. Although we should hate sin, we should never hate ourselves because we sin. God hates sin, but He loves sinners!

Only a mature believer is able to squarely face his sin and not feel condemned. We know that sin is a reality, and one that we deal with daily, so how can we deal with it and not be consumed by the reality of it? I believe it is only by firmly believing that God is greater than our sin, and by recognizing that sin is part of the human condition.

For the wages which sin pays is death, but the [bountiful] free gift of God is eternal life through (in union with) Jesus Christ our Lord.

Romans 6:23

Since all have sinned and are falling short of the honor and glory which God bestows and receives.

[All] are justified and made upright and in right standing with God, freely and gratuitously by His grace (His unmerited favor and mercy), through the redemption which is [provided] in Christ Jesus.

Romans 3:23–24

We can see from these Scriptures that sin is a problem for everyone, but Jesus is also the answer for everyone. No problem is really a problem as long as there is an answer for it. Not only have we fallen short of the glory of God, but according to Romans 3:23, we are currently falling short. This indicates it is a continual problem, yet Jesus is continually at the right hand of the Father, making intercession for us, so this continual problem of sin has a continual and uninterrupted answer. Hallelujah!

Every day our determination should be to not sin. I started my day asking for God's help in living a righteous life. I talked with Him about several things that are weaknesses for me. I asked Him to strengthen me, that I might only think thoughts and speak words that are pleasing to Him. I prayed that I might not be deceived by the devil, or be drawn into any of his traps. I don't merely take it for granted that I won't sin; I ask for God's help.

According to *Vine's Complete Expositionary Dictionary of Old and New Testament Words*, to sin means "to miss the mark." It is the most common term for moral obliquity (deviating from a right line). Sin is an act of disobedience to divine law, a trespass. Other terms for sin include disobedience, error, fault, iniquity, transgressions and ungodliness. The Bible states that whatever is not of faith is sin (Romans 14:23). Wow! That takes in a lot of things for most of us. Anything we choose to do with any attitude other than complete faith is sin. No wonder we need to be continually forgiven. I am sure glad that Jesus has already taken care of the sin problem, aren't you?

Although I deal with sin, I am not focused on it. I strongly urge you not to be either. We never overcome sin by focusing on it. When we are convicted of sin, we should admit it, repent and then turn toward Jesus. By focusing on Him and His Word, we will receive the power to overcome. For instance, if a person has a terrible temper, it won't help him to continually focus on his temper, but it will help if he meditates on the fact that Jesus has already given him His peace (John 14:27). Instead of thinking, "I am an angry person with a bad temper," he can think, "I have the peace of God dwelling in me and I am going to let it rule and lead in my life" (Colossians 3:15).

God's Word teaches us to turn away from all that will distract us unto Jesus, who is the Author and Finisher of our faith (Hebrews 12:2). The apostle Paul teaches that if we walk in the Spirit, we will not fulfill the lusts of the flesh. Always focus and meditate on doing right, not on what you have done wrong, but don't ignore sin.

One problem that man has is ignoring his sin and the other is focusing on it. We must deal with it swiftly and trust God to help us overcome it. I am concerned today that the attitude many take toward sin is unbiblical and even dangerous. Lots of people don't even refer to their sin as sin. It is their hang-up, problem, bondage, addiction or in some cases, their right. For example, we often hear that it is each individual's right to say whatever he wants to say whenever he wants to say it. We call it freedom of speech. But God clearly tells us to bridle our tongue and not speak evil things. Some feel it is a woman's right to terminate a pregnancy by getting an abortion, but God clearly tells us that children are a blessing from the Lord and only He can give and take away life.

We cannot make up our own rules about what is right or wrong to suit our preferred lifestyles, and still expect God's blessings to abound in the world.

We see the results of this loose attitude toward sin in our society today. We are living in an increasingly immoral society that has many serious problems. I have seen such decline in just fifty years that I frankly cannot imagine what our world will be like in another fifty years unless people wake up and return to God and His ways.

We cannot be responsible for what everyone else does, but we must be responsible for our own attitude, and it is important to me that I make it clear that our attitude toward sin must be the same as God's. He hates it; it grieves Him and His intention is that we progressively work with Him to overcome it, at the same time knowing that He loves us unconditionally and is always ready and willing to forgive and strengthen us. God doesn't want us to make excuses for our sin, but He does want us to face it and let Him set us free.

How to Handle Temptation

If the devil just wouldn't tempt us, things would be a lot easier. But that is not ever going to happen, so we need to stay one step ahead of him. Temptation is a part of life. Jesus in His model prayer told His disciples to pray that they would not come into temptation. He did not tell them to pray that they would never be tempted, because He knows that is not possible. But He did tell them to pray that when they were tempted, they would be able to resist.

Jesus was tempted in all points like us. He was tempted by the devil while He spent forty days and nights in the wilderness

(Luke 4). The apostle James tells us that the man is blessed who "ENDURETH temptation: for when he is tried, he shall receive the crown of life" (James 1:12 KJV). I like to say that to endure means to outlast the devil! He brings pressure on us hoping we will cave in to the temptation to do the wrong thing, and our part is to resist him in the power of the Holy Spirit.

Temptation is not sin! This is very important for us to believe. If we see each temptation as sin, we may feel that we are terrible people filled with ungodly desires. Just today someone irritated me, and I was tempted to go and tell someone else about it. I really wanted to, but I knew that God would have me keep my mouth shut and cover the offender's weakness. I continued wanting to repeat what I had seen on and off for a few hours, but as I steadfastly resisted, the urge became weaker and finally left me. Am I a bad person because I wanted to spread a rumor? No, it was actually a victory for me that I didn't give in to the temptation. We are tempted in many ways on a regular basis. God's Word teaches us that there is no temptation that comes to us that is not common to man or that is beyond human resistance, but that God is faithful and He always provides a way out (1 Corinthians 10:13).

We all have things that are temptations to us. For some it is one thing and for another it is something else. I am never tempted to rob a grocery store, but I am tempted to say things I shouldn't say, or to be impatient, as well as other things. It is good to know our own weaknesses so we can pray ahead of time to be strengthened before we are faced with the temptation. One person may be tempted in the area of sex or lying or using foul language, and another may be tempted to buy things he cannot afford to pay for, or to cheat on his income tax, or to ignore a commitment. The list of temptations that the devil is a master at is endless, but I urge you to remember that temptation is not in itself sin. It only becomes a problem if we give in to it and allow it to give birth to sin (James 1:12–15).

If the temptation is continual and tormenting, then it may require some help or ministry, but daily normal temptations are part of life. The devil tempts us, we resist him and he goes away to wait for a more opportune time to try again (Luke 4:13).

Trials That Tempt Us

Temptation comes in many forms, and one of the ways it comes is during trials and tribulations. We are often tempted to give up, or have a bad attitude, or become angry with other people. These bad attitudes should be resisted in God's power. We always see our true character clearly in difficult times. God told the Israelites that He led them forty years in the wilderness in order to humble and test them, to see if they would keep His commands (Deuteronomy 8). It is easy to think that we would behave a certain way when there is no pressure on us, but to be tested and pass the test proves the true character of a man. Jesus passed all of His tests, and prayerfully we are passing more and more of ours all the time. We know that we won't have a perfect record, but one good thing about God's testing method is that He never gives up on us and we get as many "do-overs" as we need.

Although God does test us, He never tempts us to sin. According to Scripture, we are tempted when we are enticed by our own evil desires, lust and passions (James 1:13–14). We might say that trials definitely show us our weak areas, and that can be a good thing, because anything brought out into the light can be dealt with.

Many people don't know themselves at all and they think more highly of themselves than they should. I can remember seeing others give in to temptation and thinking pridefully, "I would never do that." But when I was tested by my circumstances, I found that I had weaknesses I did not know I had. Getting to know my weaknesses allows me to pray ahead of time for God's continual strength in resisting them. The more we lean on God, the more victory we will enjoy.

Jesus Resisted Temptation

In the garden of Gethsemane, Jesus felt tremendous pressure and temptation to run from the will of God. He prayed so intensely that He sweated great drops of blood. That is some serious praying. He prayed through to victory and eventually said that although He preferred to be delivered from the things that were ahead, He was willing to submit to His Father's will in all things. This gives us a good example to follow. That we don't want to do a thing that God asks us to do does not mean that we may be excused from doing it. Pressing through and doing what is right, especially when we don't feel like it, develops spiritual maturity in us.

Jesus wanted His disciples to help Him pray, but they slept. He knew that they, too, would be tempted, and He wanted them to be strengthened ahead of time, but they slept. I wonder how many of us sleep when we should be up a little earlier, being strengthened against the temptations that the devil has planned for us that day. Jesus said, "The spirit indeed is willing, but the flesh is weak" (Matthew 26:41). We may want to do the right thing, but due to weakness in the flesh we cannot assume that we will. We dare not trust ourselves too much, but instead we should lean heavily on God to be our strength.

If Peter had prayed, perhaps he could have avoided the trauma of denying Christ three times.

Use Precautions

The book of Psalms begins by instructing the reader not to sit inactive in the pathway of sinners. If we are not aggressively resisting sin, we just might get sucked into it. Passivity or inactivity is a very dangerous thing. We must exercise our will to choose what is right and not merely assume that we can sit with evil persons and not be infected. This does not mean that we must avoid sinners altogether. The truth is that they need our presence and witness in their lives, but we do need to be careful. I always say let's be sure that we are affecting them and that they are not infecting us.

The apostle Paul told the Corinthians not to associate too closely with those who were not living right (1 Corinthians 5:9–11). A casual relationship may be acceptable, but not an intimate one. You can be friendly with someone at work who lives an immoral lifestyle, but to form an intimate and regular association would not be wise.

Another thing we should avoid is feeling superior when we see other people sinning, because this wrong attitude opens a door for a moral fall on our part (Galatians 6:1).

> Therefore let anyone who thinks he stands [who feels sure that he has a steadfast mind and is standing firm], take heed lest he fall [into sin].
>
> 1 Corinthians 10:12

This Scripture always reminds me that we are usually not quite as strong as we might like to think we are. We should pray for those we see sinning and say, "But for the grace of God, there go I." The moment we think, "I would never do that," is the moment we invite the devil into our lives to embarrass and shock us with our own behavior.

We are to avoid even the very appearance of evil (1 Thessalonians 5:22). We should live carefully. Not fearfully, but carefully. We can live large and free lives, enjoying a great deal of liberty, and at the same time live carefully. We take care in how we relate to the opposite sex, especially when one or both parties are married. For example, I once had a male employee who started bringing doughnuts each morning for one of the female employees. They were both married, and his actions made me feel uncomfortable. I told him that if he wanted to bring doughnuts, he could bring them for everyone, but not to single out one woman to show favor to. By confronting this situation, I may have saved both of them from something more tragic down the road.

Make no provision for the flesh (Romans 13:14). If you don't want to bake a cake and eat it, then don't have a cake mix in the house. If you don't want to eat dessert, don't go to the bakery and stare at all the baked goods.

If a man was previously addicted to pornography, it would be wise for him to be accountable to someone about which websites he could access on his computer. He should even avoid looking at pictures in advertising magazines sent to his home that may contain pictures of women in scanty underwear. We must be aggressive against temptation and never merely assume that we won't have a problem. God tells us to turn entirely away from evil, so we dare not flirt with it, thinking it won't be a problem for us.

Keep things off your mind that could turn into problems for you. It is dangerous to think that as long as something is only in your thoughts, it is not a real problem. All real problems start in the mind. We can never do a thing unless we first think the thing!

At the same time that the devil is tempting us to do evil, God is tempting us to do good. Which temptation will you give in to? We are dead to sin, but sin is not dead. It is alive and well on planet earth, and it must be dealt with. Resist sin and yield to righteousness. Be a channel for God to work through instead of providing the devil with an instrument to use for sin. When you make a mistake, receive God's forgiveness and press on, but don't ever be satisfied to merely stay the way that you are.

God is for progress! Enjoy where you are on the way to where you are going, but do make sure that you are going somewhere! I certainly make mistakes every day, but I have also come a long way. I don't do nearly as much wrong as I did ten years ago or five years ago or even last year, and I don't expect to be doing as much wrong this time next year as I do now. I am focused forward. I let go of what lies behind and press toward better things, and I believe that is your attitude, too. Jesus won't be disappointed in us at His second coming if we have not arrived yet, but He would be sad if He didn't find us pressing on!

CHAPTER 19

Getting Comfortable with God

All who confess that Jesus is the Son of God have God liv-ing in them, and they live in God.

1 John 4:15 (NLT)

God wants us to feel at home with Him. His Word tells us that we are His home and He is our home. Almost everyone is comfortable in his own home. It is the place where we can kick our shoes off, put on comfy clothes and be ourselves. Are you comfortable with God? Are you comfortable with yourself? You should be, and if you're not, then let's locate the problem.

We won't be comfortable with God if we fear that He is angry with us. I hope we have established that He is not angry and can put that behind us. We won't be comfortable with God if we have a wrong fear of Him. We hear about the fear of the Lord, and some are in danger of misunderstanding it. We are not to be scared of God, for there is nothing to be scared of. Nothing can separate us from His love, and He has promised to never leave us or forsake us. Fearing God properly means having such a reverence for Him that it has a great impact on the way we live our lives. The fear of God is respecting Him, obeying Him, submitting to His discipline, and worshipping Him in awe. The reverential fear of God means that we know He is powerful and always just and right in all of His ways.

How can we find the balance between entering boldly before the throne of grace and yet maintaining a fear of God? It is quite simple if we understand what a right fear is and what a wrong fear is. To fear God is one thing, but to be afraid of God is quite another.

There seems to be a tendency in Christian culture to go to extremes. One view of God lacks respect (or proper fear) and refers to Jesus as "my homeboy" or sees God as no more than a cosmic Santa Claus. Yet another view depicts Him as legalistic, exacting and almost impossible to please. No fear versus paranoia. Both are wrong.

We want to seek a proper reverence and awe for God in contrast to a terror of God.

It took me a long time to be able to honestly say that I am comfortable with God. It is a wonderful feeling and one that I never want to lose. Spending time with God for me is like being in front of a fireplace in my most comfy pajamas. I can be honest with Him, and I can let Him be honest with me. I can be totally me, with no pretense or fear of being rejected.

Tell God Everything

I encourage you to talk with God about absolutely everything. You can tell Him how you feel, what you desire and what your goals are. Tell Him what you love about Him and about your life, and express your gratitude for all that He has done for you. You can tell Him about the things in your life that you don't like or that are hard for you. Tell Him what you have done that is wrong, and talk with Him about all your concerns for yourself, your life and your loved ones. You can tell God absolutely anything and

He is never shocked or surprised because He knew all about it before you ever did it.

I don't recommend a complaining session, but I do recommend honesty. God knows exactly how we feel anyway, so not telling Him isn't keeping it from Him. We need to verbalize for our own sake. We need to vent, or to express ourselves, and it is always better to do it with God than with anyone else.

> God knows exactly how we feel anyway, so not telling Him isn't keeping it from Him. We need to verbalize for our own sake. We need to vent, or to express ourselves, and it is always better to do it with God than with anyone else.

You may find solutions to your problems more easily if you're more honest and open about them. Also, be sure to listen to what God tells you either through His Word or as a direct revelation to your heart. Communication is a two-way street. It doesn't consist of one person doing all the talking while the other does all the listening. You may have to develop an ability to listen as I did. I was always better at talking than I was at listening, but God has some very awesome things to say if we learn to hear Him.

God has invited us into a relationship of fellowship with Him. It is to be an intimate relationship in which we share absolutely everything.

God is not someone we visit for one hour on Sunday morning and ignore the rest of the week unless we have an emergency. He is someone we live with. He is our home and we must be comfortable with Him.

Religion will drive us mad! By religion I mean a system that gives us rules and regulations to follow and prescribes punishments when we fail. If we pursue God through religion, we are doomed to fail, because not one of us can follow all the rules, and in due time we get tired of punishing ourselves and we simply give up. My father had a lot of rules and I never knew which ones he was enforcing on any given day; therefore, I felt tense in his presence, because I never knew when I might be doing the wrong thing. I am grateful for the freedom I enjoy in my relationship with God. One that is available for each one of us.

Trust God at All Times

Good relationships are built on trust, and God wants us to choose to trust Him with ourselves and everything else in our lives. God is faithful and it is impossible for Him to fail us. We might perceive something to be a failure if we don't get what we want, but God cannot fail. He may have something better in mind for us and we simply don't know how to ask for it yet. God only has our benefit and well-being in His plan for us, and the best policy is to always relax and trust Him.

I believe that God trusts us. I don't think He feels tension thinking about what we may or may not do. He knows everything about us before we are even born and He still invites us to be in relationship with Him. He told Jeremiah that before he was born, He knew and approved of him as His chosen instrument (Jeremiah 1:5). How can that be? Jeremiah wasn't perfect; in fact he dealt with fear and insecurity. God doesn't require that we be perfect; His only requirement is that we believe in Him, which is another way of saying that we trust Him. If we will give God our total trust, there are no limits to what He can do through us and for us.

Trust God's ways and His timing. They are not like ours, but they are never in error. God is usually not early, but He is truly never late. His timing is impeccable. Quite often God could lead us on an easier route in taking us where He wants us to end up, but He may choose a longer or harder route because there are things we need to learn along the way. Let us learn to thank God for all the times in our life and for every season. Winter is just as valuable as spring. All things work together for good to those who love God and are called according to His purpose (Romans 8:28). Being able to believe this one verse of Scripture will release you into unimaginable rest and peace.

Trust is a beautiful thing, and it saves us a great deal of emotional and mental turmoil. Suspicious fear is an open doorway to torment. Trust is something we decide to do, not something we necessarily feel. Any time we trust a person we realize that we may get disappointed or hurt, but when we decide to trust God, that is not the case. Trust is what makes a relationship comfortable. We put our money in a bank because it has a good reputation and we decide to trust our money to it. God has a much better reputation than even the best bank in the world, so we can surely decide to deposit ourselves with Him and put our total trust in His Word.

Just think, you can always trust God with your secrets. He won't tell anybody! You can trust Him to always understand everything about you, because He understands you better than you understand yourself. You can trust Him to never reject you, to always be there for you, to be on your side and to love you unconditionally. He is merciful, long-suffering with our weaknesses and more patient than we can even fathom.

Truly we can say, "What a Friend we have in Jesus."

I believe the proper fear of the Lord begins with trusting Him and grows from there.

It grows until it consumes one's whole life.

Paul David Tripp said, "To fear God means that my life is structured by a sense of awe, worship, and obedience that flows out of recognizing Him and His glory. He becomes the single most important reference point for all that I desire, think, do and say. God is my motive and God is my goal. The fear of God is meant to be the central organizing force in my life."

God is everything and we are nothing without Him! He is a consuming fire (Hebrews 12:29). He consumes everything in us that is not consistent with His will and sets everything else on fire for His glory. Are you ready for that kind of surrender? If so, then you have a healthy fear of God!

No Rooms Closed Off

We often see rooms in a house that always have the door closed and no one goes in or out. If it is not our home, we may wonder what is behind that door. Is it something that no one is allowed to see? Is it useless storage that no one has the courage to get rid of? Is it a room filled with secrets? Do you have any rooms in your life that are closed to God? When God touches certain things in your life, do you say, "Oh, no, God, not that!" We cannot be totally comfortable with God and have secret areas that we keep closed off to Him. He won't force His way into those areas, but He does want to be trusted enough to be invited.

For many years I kept the room of my sexual abuse closed to God. I didn't think about it or talk about it. It was always there right beneath the surface of my thoughts and emotions, but I kept it suppressed. The time came when God was ready for me to deal with it, and at first I flatly said, "No, I won't deal with that." I had a book in my hand detailing another woman's story that mirrored mine, and as I read, it brought memories to the surface I didn't want to look at. I threw the book across the room and said, "I will not read this book," and God said, "It is time!"

When God says that it is time to deal with something, then the time is right even if we don't feel that it is. That day I started to open the door to a room that had been closed for many years, and although it was painful and hard, it turned out to be the best thing I ever did. Our secrets can make us sick, and God wants us to be whole, so be sure that you invite Him into every room in your life.

We don't have to be afraid that God will see something that will make Him angry or that will shock Him. His desire is to walk through the room with you and bring healing to you along the way. As I walked through the sexual abuse of my past, I had to confront things that I had hidden from for a long time. I had to confront my dad and my mother. We had never talked about the secret in our home, and it was making us all sick. I would like to say that I was met with honesty and apologies, but instead I was met with excuses, blame and anger. It didn't turn out the way I wanted it to until many years later, but I had done the part that God had asked me to do and that started a healing in my soul.

I had to face the sad fact that my parents did not love me as parents should love a child, and more than likely they would never be able to do so properly. I recall looking at myself in the mirror and saying out loud, "Joyce, your parents don't, and never did love you, but God does. It is time to enjoy what you do have and stop trying to get something you will never have." That was a sort of release for me. It is a waste of time to try to get something that they simply were incapable of giving me.

There were many things like this that God led me through over the next few years, but His timing was always perfect and each step brought a little more healing and freedom. I strongly encourage you to let God into every room in your life, and especially the ones you are not proud of, or are afraid to face.

When we fear God properly, we will never deny Him access to any area of our lives that He wants to be part of. The fear of the Lord is the beginning of knowledge (Proverbs 1:7). We have not even begun to know anything until we accept God's rightful place in our lives and out of respect and awe submit our wills to Him in all things.

Are you still trying to run your own life? If so, you are headed for a disaster. Put God in the driver's seat and enjoy the ride. When we put God first among all of our priorities, He will make our lives better.

Surrender

I am learning to love the word "surrender." It means that I stop wrestling with God and resisting His will. I may not like all that He is doing or the way He is doing it, but I can surrender. I can yield, and so can you. Some of the things that hurt us in life could stop hurting if we would embrace them rather than constantly resisting them.

Mary's husband suddenly died and she was devastated, to say the least. Her pain was tragic and four years after his death she was still hurting just as much as she was in the beginning. She had become depressed, isolated and bitter because life had seemingly not been fair to her. Mary was on a downhill slide and she had a decision to make. She could go on resisting what she obviously could not change, or she could change her mind and decide to embrace it and trust God to work good out of it. When we continue to resist something that we obviously cannot do anything about, it makes us miserable, but we can surrender and embrace the circumstance, and even though it still hurts, the surrender will allow healing to begin. We can find a new beginning, a fresh place to start. We cannot move on to where we would like to be if we refuse to face where we are!

> *We cannot move on to where we would like to be if we refuse to face where we are!*

John lost his job after thirty-five years with the company. He was angry, and that anger ate at him until it started affecting all of his personal relationships. He sank deeper and deeper into self-pity and depression. What could he do? The only healthy things John could do were to surrender to the circumstance, accept it and see it as an opportunity for a new beginning. He ended up starting a small business of his own and enjoyed more freedom and financial prosperity than ever before, but things could have turned out quite differently. Had John continued to refuse to surrender to the situation with a good attitude, he could have lost much more than his job.

The attitude of yielding is also helpful in daily situations that tend to frustrate us. Let's say that I am scheduled on a flight and when I arrive I find that it has been delayed and no one knows for how long. I can sit and be frustrated, complaining about the airlines the entire time, or I can surrender to the circumstance I obviously cannot do anything about and enjoy the wait. I can do something creative or I can get some work done that I need to do. Either way, I am going to be waiting, and it is up to me what kind of attitude I wait with.

Is there anything in your life that you simply need to surrender to and trust God with? If so, don't put it off. The longer you wait, the longer you will stay miserable!

Any time we resist what only God can control, we get out of the comfort zone with Him. To be comfortable with God requires walking in step with Him, not pushing against Him. It requires surrender, not resistance.

For many years I was uncomfortable with God, but fortunately I can say today that I am totally comfortable. I am not afraid of Him, but I do have reverential fear. I trust Him enough to submit to what I cannot control and embrace whatever He permits in my life. I pray that you will also find and enjoy that place of comfort. God is your lifetime partner, so being comfortable with Him should be a priority in your life.

CHAPTER 20

Spiritual Growth

If a man does not exercise his arm, he develops no muscle; and if a man does not exercise his soul, he acquires no muscle in his soul, no strength of character, no vigor of moral fiber, nor beauty of spiritual growth.

Henry Drummond

Perhaps you have a lovely home. One that is beautiful and even admired by those who pass by and see it. People see the home, but they don't see the foundation. However, the foundation is the most important part of the home, because without it the home would not be standing.

Many Christians try to build a life, one that is powerful and to be admired, but they have not taken time to build a strong foundation and their life keeps falling apart. This is what I did for many years, and the same thing might be the case with you. I received Christ as my Savior and started immediately trying to do good works. I tried to serve in church on various committees, I tried to be patient, I tried to love people, and many other noble things. In other words, I was trying to build a spiritual life and display godly character, but I failed to realize that I did not have a solid foundation yet. I did not know the unconditional love of God for me, I felt guilty and condemned most of the time, I did not know how to receive God's mercy, I did not understand the doctrine of righteousness and I definitely felt that God was mad at me. I could not experience spiritual growth without the foundation I needed.

I have spent nineteen chapters in this book teaching you how to make sure that you have a solid foundation in your own life, and now it is time to talk about building a life that will glorify God. It is time to discuss spiritual growth.

The understanding of grace, forgiveness, mercy, the unconditional love of God and the doctrine of righteousness through Christ is the foundation for everything else in our relationship with and service to God. We must be rooted deeply in the unconditional love of God, know with certainty that His attitude toward us is merciful and have revelation of who we are "in Christ." We must have an understanding of our being the righteousness of God in Christ and not be afraid that God is angry when we make mistakes. Once those things are established facts, it is natural that we will have a desire to press on to becoming all that God wants us to be. We will have a desire for spiritual growth.

The apostle Paul in the book of Hebrews told the people that it was time for them to get past the elementary or beginning stages in the teachings and doctrines of Christ and that they needed to go on to spiritual maturity.

> *Therefore let us go on and get past the elementary stage in the teachings and doctrine of Christ (the Messiah), advancing steadily toward the completeness and perfection that belong to spiritual maturity.*
>
> Hebrews 6:1

Paul told the Hebrew Christians that although they should be teaching others by now, they still needed someone to teach them over again the first principles of God's Word. They apparently kept needing to hear the same messages over and over about foundational things and were unable or unwilling to go on to other teachings that would help them build a life through which they could glorify and serve God.

> *For even though by this time you ought to be teaching others, you actually need someone to teach you over again the very first principles of God's Word. You have come to need milk, not solid food.*
>
> *For everyone who continues to feed on milk is obviously inexperienced and unskilled in the doctrine of righteousness (of conformity to the divine will in purpose, thought, and action), for he is a mere infant [not able to talk yet]!*
>
> Hebrews 5:12–13

He told them they still needed the milk of the Word and not solid food. They were not able to handle the meat of the Word. What is the meat of the Word? I believe it is teaching about spiritual maturity, sacrifice, obedience, unselfish living and service to God and man. It is always easy and enjoyable to hear messages about God's love for us and the amazing plan He has for our lives, but it might not be as easy or enjoyable to hear about doing the will of God even if it requires personal sacrifice. The truth is that we need both in order to be healthy, productive believers in Christ.

God's Word encourages and comforts us. It teaches us who we are in Christ and about His amazing grace, forgiveness and love, but it also chastises and corrects us. When Paul was mentoring Timothy, he told him that as a preacher of God's Word, he was to show people in what way their lives are wrong. He was to convince them, rebuke and correct them, warn and urge and encourage them (2 Timothy 4:2).

Are You Drinking Milk and Eating Meat?

Most of what I said in the first nineteen chapters of this book was all very encouraging, but I would not be giving you a complete picture of God's will for us if I did not also tell you that in building a life that will glorify God you will need to let the Word of God correct you and lead you in all your actions. I believe the milk of the Word is the encouraging messages that we all need and love, and that the meat of the Word deals with our behavior and spiritual maturity. Actually, both milk and meat are encouraging. One encourages us to be confident in our position as God's children, and the other encourages us to serve Him and bear good fruit for His Kingdom.

As a teacher of God's Word for thirty-five years, I have witnessed over and over again how many people are quite happy to receive the milk of the Word, but they choke on the meat. They love to be encouraged, but they won't submit to rebuke or correction. The result is that they have a wonderful foundation, but they never go on to build a life that will bring glory to God. I believe you are ready and willing to go on to spiritual maturity. I believe that you are someone who desires to walk in God's will in all things.

The milk of the Word teaches us all that God has done for us in Christ, freely by His grace, and that our part is to only receive and enjoy. Just as a baby drinks only milk for quite a while because he is unable to digest other things, the baby Christian needs this milk of God's Word. However, if a baby never drank anything but milk, he would never grow into a healthy adult. He needs milk and meat and so do we as Christians.

The apostle Paul said that the people continued to feed on milk because they were unskilled in the doctrine of righteousness (Hebrews 5:12–13). They still did not truly know who they were in Christ. They did not understand that they had been made the righteousness of God in Christ; therefore, when Paul tried to correct them with the Word, or confront their childish behavior, they responded unfavorably. They could not receive correction through the Word of God without feeling condemned.

It is vital that we know our position in Christ, for if we truly know who we are, then when the Word of God confronts what we do (behavior), it doesn't condemn us. We can receive it as another level of God's love chastising us for our own good.

When conviction from the Holy Spirit immediately turns into condemnation in our thinking, the process of change is halted and no spiritual growth takes place. We must be mature enough to know that God's chastisement is a display of His love, of His being unwilling to let us alone in our sinful condition.

> *Those whom I [dearly and tenderly] love, I tell their faults and convict and convince and reprove and chasten [I discipline and instruct them]. So be enthusiastic and in earnest and burning with zeal and repent [changing your mind and attitude].*
>
> Revelation 3:19

God doesn't seek to change us so He can love us; His love is unconditional and not based on our behavior, but we should seek to change because we love Him. God wants us to be fruitful! He wants our lives to add value to the lives of other people and for our example in the world to draw people into the Kingdom of God.

I have four grown children, and for the foundation-laying years of their life (childhood, adolescence and young adulthood), Dave and I did everything for them. We provided all of their needs, clothed, educated, fed, housed and loved them with all of our might. During that time we also taught and corrected them. We encouraged them a lot, but we also corrected them, and any parents who don't do so do not really love their children. We were preparing them for a life that would be enjoyable and fruitful. As they matured, they began to do things for us as well as receive from us, and it kept our relationships healthy. This is the natural progression of relationship and must also happen in our relationship with God.

Are you ready to mature and say to God, "I am thankful that You love me. I appreciate all You have done for me, and now I want to serve You; I want to do things for You; I want to bear good fruit for You"? Are you ready to ask God to mold you into the image of Jesus Christ and show you how to build a life on the foundation He has given you that will bring Him glory? If your answer is yes, and I believe that it is, you will need to start receiving the meat of God's Word.

Not All Christians Are Mature

Paul confronted Christians who were not maturing. He said, "Brothers and sisters, I could not address you as people who live by the Spirit but as people who are still worldly—mere infants in Christ. I gave you milk, not solid food, for you were not yet ready for it. Indeed, you are still not ready" (1 Corinthians 3:1–2 NIV).

Paul speaks of two types of Christians. The first is the spiritual man who is able to examine, investigate, inquire into and discern all things. He is able to quickly discern good from evil and he chooses the good. Then Paul speaks of the carnal Christian, one who is regenerated in Christ (he is born again), yet he remains in the infancy stage of spiritual growth. He has the nature of the flesh and follows the lead of ordinary impulses (1 Corinthians 2:14–16).

I wasted many years of my Christian experience as a carnal, fleshly, immature believer. I had some understanding of salvation by grace, but I truly did not have the solid foundation that I needed. After God helped me build that foundation, I still spent many years in immaturity because I had not made the decision to go on to spiritual maturity. I don't believe anyone experiences spiritual growth unless he truly desires it. I finally became dissatisfied with my life as it was and reached a crisis point in my walk with God. Something had to change! I had been receiving from Him (love, grace, mercy, forgiveness, help) for years, but what was missing? I wondered. I saw that it was time for me to give back. I needed to give myself and everything I had to Him for His use and purpose. When I did, it was a turning point in my spiritual life and one that I have never regretted.

I love Paul's letter to the Ephesians. He lays a solid foundation by spending the first three chapters telling people how much God loves them and what their inheritance is in Him. Then he starts Chapter 4 with this statement: "I therefore, the prisoner for the Lord, appeal to and beg you to walk (lead a life) worthy of the [divine] calling to which you have been called (with behavior that is a credit to the summons to God's service." It obviously wasn't enough to only teach people what was theirs in Christ; they also needed to be taught how to let Jesus shine through them in every aspect of their daily lives. People may go to church on Sunday, but do they take Jesus to work with them on Monday and every other day of the week? Is the Word of God ruling in their home? Is He filling their thoughts, words and actions?

Are you ready to go on to spiritual maturity? I believe you are; therefore, if you have not done so yet, put God in the driver's seat of your life. Realize that God is more interested in changing you than in changing all of your circumstances. Ask God to change you in any area where you need change! When He starts doing it, don't resist Him. Trust Him to do the work and remain in His rest.

The Salvation of the Soul

So get rid of all uncleanness and the rampant outgrowth of wickedness, and in a humble (gentle, modest) spirit receive and welcome the Word which implanted and rooted [in your hearts] contains the power to save your souls.

James 1:21

When we receive Christ as our Savior, our spirit is saved or born again. It is made holy and God comes to dwell in us. Our soul (mind, will and emotions) still needs to be renewed. It must be turned over to God for His use. If it is not, the world will never see Jesus shining through us.

The Word of God, when it is truly received and becomes rooted in our hearts, does have the power to save our souls, as James 1:21 says. We must love the Word and study it. To read it, or to hear someone else teach it, is good, but it is not enough. We must study! Let me boldly ask you how much time you spend studying God's Word yourself. I pray that it is often, for without that, there will be very little growth.

In *The Lost Art of Disciple Making*, Leroy Eims provides a wonderful image of this phenomenon. "One spring our family was driving from Fort Lauderdale to Tampa, Florida. As far as the eye could see, orange trees were loaded with fruit. When we stopped for breakfast, I ordered orange juice with my eggs. 'I'm sorry,' the waitress said. 'I can't bring you orange juice. Our machine is broken.' At first I was dumbfounded. We were surrounded by millions of oranges, and I knew they had oranges in the kitchen—orange slices garnished our plates. What was the problem? No juice? Hardly. We were surrounded by thousands of gallons of juice. The problem was they had become dependent on a machine to get it. Christians are sometimes like that. They may be surrounded by Bibles in their homes, but if something should happen to the Sunday morning preaching service, they would have no nourishment for their souls. The problem is not a lack of spiritual food—but that many Christians haven't grown enough to know how to get it for themselves."

The Word of God is the food our spirit needs to remain strong and it renews our minds (Romans 12:2). When we learn to think right, all other things begin to go right.

Spiritual maturity does not develop from merely having knowledge of God's Word, but from applying it in everyday life and learning to live by it. Let's say that you have been studying what God's Word says about patience and you agree with it and have full intention of being patient. Now, let's say that you go shopping and a clerk waits on you who is very slow. She is new at her job and doesn't seem to know how to operate the computer properly. You are in a bit of a hurry and you can feel impatience welling up in your soul. At this point you have a decision to make. Will you behave according to the impatience you are feeling, or will you walk in the spirit and display the patience that God has given you? If you display patience, then you have exercised your "patience muscle" and it has become stronger, and you have glorified God by choosing to represent Him well.

We have God's Word readily available to us via church attendance, radio, television, the Internet, CDs, DVDs, our phone and other devices. We don't have a famine of God's Word, but we do need more people who will exercise regularly by applying the Word to their lives.

Paul exhorted Christians to work out their salvation with fear and trembling. He didn't mean that they were to work for their salvation, but that they should work with the Holy Spirit toward spiritual maturity (Philippians 2:12). He quickly goes on to tell them that it cannot be accomplished in their own strength, but that God would work in them to accomplish it.

Pursuing What Matters Most

The things that we seek or pursue tell a lot about our character. We are told to seek first the Kingdom of God and His righteousness (His way of doing and being right) (Matthew 6:33). We are told to seek peace, and in my experience I have found that the only way to have peace is to learn to promptly obey the Holy Spirit. We are also told to seek God's presence, for that is the most precious gift that we can have. We need God more than we need what He can do for us. I like to say, "Seek God's presence, not His presents."

We are also told to pursue holiness, without which no one will see the Lord (Hebrews 12:14). Wow! That could sound a bit frightening unless we understand that the thing being stressed is the pursuing. God wants us to pursue holiness even if we never arrive at the place of perfection. If we are pursuing holiness, which is another way of saying spiritual maturity, it reveals a right attitude toward God. As I said earlier in this book, we're made holy by God when we are born again. We have the holiness in our spirit that God expects us to manifest, but it will not be manifested if we are passive. We must pursue it! Pursuing holiness is another way of saying, "Work out your salvation with fear and trembling," or, "Let us go on to spiritual maturity."

> The stiff and wooden quality about religious lives is a result of our lack of holy desire. Complacency is a deadly foe for all spiritual growth. Acute desire must be present or there will be no manifestation of Christ to His people.
>
> A. W. Tozer

Holiness is not following a set of rules and regulations; it is simply and joyfully learning to follow the leading of the Holy Spirit.

> [Live] as children of obedience [to God]; do not conform yourselves to the evil desires [that governed you] in your former ignorance [when you did not know the requirements of the Gospel].
> But as the One Who called you is holy, you yourselves also be holy in all your conduct and manner of living.
> For it is written, You shall be holy, for I am holy.
>
> 1 Peter 1:14–16

God is giving us a promise that because He is holy and living in us, we can also be holy in all of our conduct and manner of living. It is a process that is worked out gradually as we continue to pursue it in the power of the Holy Spirit. Jesus won't be at all disappointed when He returns if we have not arrived, but He does want to find us pursuing holiness.

Working the Works of God

We are saved by faith alone and not by works, but James said that faith without works is dead, and it is void of power (James 2:14–18). Faith needs works (deeds and actions of obedience to back it up), otherwise it is destitute of power.

We are warned over and over in Scripture that the works of our flesh are not acceptable to God, but we are also told that we are to work the works of God. Jesus said, "I have glorified You... by completing the work that You gave Me to do" (John 17:4). Our "works" (works of the flesh) are our energy trying to do what only God can do, but God's works are works that we do at His bidding and only by His power.

We should avoid works of the flesh like the plague. They are things like trying to save ourselves, make ourselves righteous by our own works, produce good fruit by struggling, or following our human plans to get what we want instead of asking God for them and waiting on His way and timing.

Although we avoid works of the flesh, we should aggressively pursue doing the work of God. God wants all of us to obey His Word, but I also believe that He gives each of us an assignment in life. As we continue to grow in God and learn to follow the leadership of the Holy Spirit, we will learn what that assignment is. Fortunately, we don't have to compete with anyone, but we are free to be the unique individual that God designed us to be.

The assignment that God gives us may or may not seem spectacular to the world, but it is spectacular to God. You may be a mom who is raising a child who will do great things for God. Or you may be a janitor in a school and a great example of someone with godly character to the children. You could even be a very famous person, but all that really matters is whether we are ful-

filling our God-ordained assignment. When we are, we are working the works of God.

There are different seasons in our life, and our assignment
can change as those seasons change. After Dave and I married, I
spent many years doing various kinds of office work, then I had
years of being a stay-at-home mom, then I went back to work and
eventually started a Bible study where I worked and that developed into the ministry I lead today. All of that happened over a
span of forty-seven years, so I encourage you to understand that
whatever you are doing now is an important part of your life that
you should embrace and enjoy. When the seasons change, go on
the next assignment that God has for you and do it with eager-
ness and joy.

What Is the Sign of Spiritual Maturity?

I think we can simplify what spiritual maturity means by saying that it is loving people the way God does. Above all that we
pursue, we should aggressively pursue truly loving people. To be
spiritually mature means to be like God, and He loves people.

The apostle Peter exhorts us to take the promises of God and
add our diligence by employing every effort in exercising our
faith to develop virtue (excellence, resolution, Christian energy),
and in exercising virtue we develop knowledge (intelligence). He
goes on to say that as we exercise knowledge, we will develop
self-control, and in exercising self-control, we will develop steadfastness (patience, endurance). In exercising steadfastness, we
will develop godliness (piety). And in exercising godliness, we
develop brotherly affection, and in exercising brotherly affection,
we develop Christian love (2 Peter 1:3–7). We see that the end
goal is Christian love!

It looks as if we must be diligent and make an effort to keep growing if we ever expect to reach our goal of learning to love as God does. We can also see from what Peter says that reaching this goal is a process that will obviously take time. And don't forget to enjoy the journey! Our journey with God is the most exciting part of our lives.

How is true spiritual love manifested? We find the answer in 1 Corinthians 13:4–8.

Love is patient
Love is kind
Love does not envy
Love does not boast
Love is not proud
Love is not rude
Love is not self-seeking
Love is not easily angered
Love keeps no record of wrongs
Love does not delight in evil, but rejoices in the truth
Love bears up under anything that comes
Love always believes the best of everyone
Love is always full of hope in all circumstances
Love endures everything without weakening
Love never fails

I know that I need to keep exercising in these areas and pursuing holiness; how about you? I urge you to ponder your behavior and ask yourself before God what areas you might need to improve in. I know that I could be more patient and less self-seeking, just to name a couple of things. I pursue these goals with all of my heart, but I am never condemned when I don't succeed totally. I just keep pressing on. I don't feel condemned, because I have a solid foundation in my life of knowing that God loves me unconditionally, has forgiven all of my sins and is merciful, and that His grace (undeserved favor and power) are always available to me. I press past my mistakes and I keep praying and leaning on God and expecting to see Him work through me.

I find several Scriptures that tell me to examine myself. That doesn't mean that we should be excessively introspective, nor should we be judgmental toward ourselves, but taking an honest look at our behavior is healthy.

> *For if we searchingly examined ourselves [detecting our short-comings and recognizing our own condition], we should not be judged and penalty decreed [by the divine judgment].*
>
> 1 Corinthians 11:31

> *Examine and test and evaluate your own selves to see whether you are holding to your faith and showing the proper fruits of it.*
>
> 2 Corinthians 13:5

Perhaps if we were willing to be more honest with ourselves about ourselves, we would make faster progress in spiritual maturity. Let us follow the gentle prompting of the Holy Spirit concerning our behavior so we don't have to be corrected more sternly by God. God is concerned more with our spiritual growth than He is with our present comfort. The spiritually mature person can examine himself honestly in the light of God's Word and never feel condemned when he sees his flaws. He is actually delighted to see them, because he knows that only the truth makes him free. He knows that God's love for him is not based on his behavior, but he does desire to improve in order to bring more glory to God.

Spiritual maturity is not church attendance, knowledge of church doctrines, giving large sums of money to the church, holding a position on the church leadership team or being on a church committee. Spiritual maturity is not memorizing Scripture, or reading the Bible through each year. We can do religious exercises by the thousands and still not be spiritually mature.

I am not going to give you a list of things to do in order to develop spiritual maturity. I have shared the importance of studying God's Word and regular fellowship with Him, including prayer, but beyond that, the only thing I will say is...follow the leadership of the Holy Spirit. If you do, He will teach you all that you need to know and He will do it in a way that will work perfectly for you.

We all do a lot of things that are connected with our Christianity. We go to church, read the Bible, pray, read Christian books and perhaps listen to Christian radio or watch Christian television, but to what purpose?

"A while back on *The Merv Griffin Show*," says Gary Gulbranson in an article in *Leadership* magazine, "the guest was a bodybuilder. During the interview, Merv asked, 'Why do you develop those particular muscles?' The bodybuilder simply stepped forward and flexed a series of well-defined muscles from chest to calf. The audience applauded. 'What do you use all those muscles for?' Merv asked. Again, the muscular specimen flexed, and biceps and triceps sprouted to impressive proportions. 'But what do you *use* those muscles for?' Merv persisted. The bodybuilder was bewildered. He didn't have an answer other than to display his well-developed frame. I was reminded that our spiritual exercises—Bible study, prayer, reading Christian books and listening to Christian radio—are also for a purpose. They are meant to strengthen our ability to build God's Kingdom, not simply to improve our pose before an admiring audience."

I believe that God has a purpose in all the things He does, and we should also be people with a purpose. When we study or hear preaching, let it always be with the purpose of doing what we have learned. If we hear but don't do, we deceive ourselves by reasoning that is contrary to the truth (James 1:22).

I am called by God to help the believers mature and grow up spiritually so they can be all God wants them to be, do all that God wants them to do and have all that God wants them to have. That is my assignment! No message from me would be complete without some teaching on how to walk out your faith in your everyday life. I want you to press forward and grow, but I don't want you to ever think that God is angry with you when you make mistakes. God loves you, and He is patient and long-suffering. He is always there to pick you up when you fall down and help you get started in the right direction again. God will never give up on you!

Do you wish this wasn't the end?
Are you hungry for more great teaching, inspiring
testimonies, ideas to challenge your faith?

Join us at www.hodderfaith.com, follow us on Twitter
or find us on Facebook to make sure you get the latest from
your favourite authors.

Including interviews, videos, articles, competitions
and opportunities to tell us just what you thought about
our latest releases.